'FLOW BLUE CHINA
the Comprehensive Guide

Identification

and

Values

Mary Frank Gaston

COLLECTOR BOOKS
A Division of Schroeder Publishing Co., Inc.

On the cover:
Gloire de Dijon, Doulton, circa 1891 – 1902,
Wash Bowl and Pitcher. $2,500.00 – 3,000.00 set.
Photograph courtesy of Steve Kimbriel.

Cover design by Beth Summers
Book design by Allan Ramsey

Collector Books
P.O. Box 3009
Paducah, KY 42002-3009
www.collectorbooks.com

Copyright © 2005 Mary Frank Gaston

The current values in this book should be used only as a guide.
They are not intended to set prices, which vary from one section of the
country to another. Auction prices as well as dealer prices vary greatly and
are affected by condition as well as demand. Neither the author nor the
publisher assumes responsibility for any losses that might be incurred as a
result of consulting this guide.

Searching For A Publisher?

We are always looking for people knowledgeable within their fields. If
you feel that there is a real need for a book on your collectible subject and
have a large comprehensive collection, contact Collector Books.

Contents

Dedication

To Jerry and Jeremy

Acknowledgments

A very large number of collectors and dealers have helped me produce my three books about Flow Blue China over the last 20 plus years. Without their contributions, not only with photographs and information, but also with their interest in sharing their finds and collections with others, these books could not have been written. I sincerely thank each and every one.

Contributors to *Gaston's Flow Blue China*

Gerald Abell
Tom Ammann
Jeanette Anderson
Danielle Arnet
Eleanore Ashworth
Helene Augenblick
Martha Bailey
Sheril and Steve Bailey
Peg Banks
Banowetz Antiques,
Virl and Kathy Banowetz and
    Frantzen Photography
Gosin Bement
Patricia Bennett
Bette Bird
Mrs. Daryl Black
Naomi Blom
Sue and George Bosu
Pat Buteau
Sérgio Paula Souza Caiuby
Sonya Carlson
Carolyn Cash
Mark Chervenka
Mike and Judy Cleary
Phyllis P. Collins
Patricia L. Daniel
Betty Dassett

Mary C. Dean
Jane Del Savio
Julie Dolan
Marilyn Dufresne
Shireen E. Ebner
Kathryn Elliott
Brenda Fricke
Barbara Gibbs
C. E. Gockel
Rosalind Goldstein
Debbie Goyogana
Judy and Ernie Grant
Bernice H. Gray
Debby Hagara
Rosemary L. Hall
Hazel Harp
Audrey M. Harris
Brian Heath
Carolyn Hegadorn
Christopher Charles Hohns
Liz Jaffe
Sue and Robert Jones
Phyllis Kellar
Charree Kelly
Carolyn Kemble
Steve Kimbriel
Terri Kindred

Robyn Kogan
Alan Kushner
Marena Lagerstrom
Gladys Landreth
Debbie Cairns LaRue
Peter Laur
Roy T. Leitza
Evelyn and Charles Lewis
Gregory Lewis
Muriel Lindon
Elizabeth J. Lippmann
Shirley Loegering
Patricia Lucas
Wendy Lyon
James B. McClenahan, MD
Pat McNeil
Jan McQueen
David C. Metz
Amy Miller
Sandra Moorman
Judith K. Morrison
Garrison E. Moyer
Peri Muretta
Blanche Murtagh
Kathy Neshek
Lori Norris
Janet Nussberg-Makos

Kathleen O'Connor
Eduardo R. Oliva
June Otis
Ernie Pauscher
David W. Peters
Betty Peterson
John A. Porter
Dr. Tom Pruett
Sheila Ralston
Mary Ann Rapposelli
Connie Reder
Jean C. Reynolds
Mike Richards
Earl D. Rogers

J. Stewart Rogers
Bernice J. Rudell
Vivian Saunders
Ronnie Scemons
Ann Schultz
Serendipity Antiques
S. Shulman
Barbara J. Singer
Nel Slaughter
Richard Snell
Pat Speece
Mrs. Ross P. Spinney
Linda M. Stevenson
Khris Sundvahl

Stephanie L. Systema
Jane Thomasson
Gail Thurman-Lansdon
Teri Tower
Jan and Dave Truax
Veronica Tunler
Margaret Vanlier
Donn E. Welden
John T. White
Norman H. Wolfe
Connie Yore
Roberta Zamore

Contributors for *The Collector's Encyclopedia of Flow Blue China, Second Series*

Bill and Sandy Alley
Susan Anastasio
F. R. Anderson
Carleen André-Rogers
Jeanette Bader
Marla Betz
Martha Card
Clara R. Casper
June Chance
Nancy Cottrell
Betty DeKeyser
Betty French
JuDeane Garrett
Richard C. and Sondra Green
Peggy Grotts
Merle and Grace Harris
Freda Hines
Margaret Hoeft
Rajayne Hoffmann

Claire M. Hopkins
Horseshoe Antiques
Malorie Hunt
Tim and Janis Hunt
Betty Hurley
Lorraine Kohlbeck
Becky Korbel
Pam and Ralph Krainik
Shirley Krantzberg
Fern and Joseph Krisman
Ruth Lehman
Kim McKinney
Virginia Metcalf
Mrs. E. R. Meyersick
M. Clydene Miles
Earlene Moore
Richard Muscott
Helen Nelson
Elta Oslon

James S. Pitcher
Lawrence R. Reno
Jean Riecker
Shirley Seitz
Cindie Smith
Sue and C. Aubrey Smith, Jr.
Danell Smith-Wright
Theva C. Stevens
Dave Taylor
Doris L. Thompson
David Turner
Patricia Brophy Wall and
    Patterson Wall
Charles and Dorothy Washer
Viginia Avis Whitham
Brad and Eunice Witt
Diana and Ted Wood
Juanita Zinn

Contributors to *The Collector's Encyclopedia of Flow Blue China*

Joyce Brown
Dorothy and Elmer Caskey
Crawford's Antiques
Mr. and Mrs. Phil Cummins
David Dodgen
Gladys M. Donham
Dunn & Ross Antiques
Arvena Fleury
Georgia Harris
Professor and Mrs. William L. Hendricks
Charlene and Don Johnson

Suzanne King
Irene and Marc Luther
Vera McLeod
Lois Misiewicz
Carolyn and Max Allen Nickerson
Shirley Porter
Connie Rogers
Floris and Carl Walton
Lloyd Ward Antique Shows
Marceline White

Preface

Over 20 years ago I wrote my first book about Flow Blue China. Thanks to collector interest, I was able to publish a *Second Series* in 1994. This new 2005 edition expands the material of those earlier guides. Eight hundred pictures of Flow Blue patterns are shown, combining examples from my earlier books with new patterns and pieces to give collectors a more comprehensive guide. A value range is quoted for each piece. Because of the growth of new "flow blue" on the market, the section on Reproductions has been enlarged and can be found as the last section of this book.

Marks for over 100 companies, including English and non-English manufacturers, are shown. The marks are from my previous books plus additional marks for some of the companies. Many new marks have also been included for companies represented for the first time in this edition. The marks are separated into English and non-English sections. With the manufacturers' marks, I have listed the Flow Blue patterns made by each company represented in this book. This serves as a pattern and manufacturer index.

Although the factory marks are separated into English and non-English sections, for collector convenience, the English and non-English Flow Blue patterns are grouped together and illustrated in alphabetical order. Manufacturer's names, marks, and approximate dates or time periods for the production of the particular pattern are listed in the captions for the patterns.

I hope collectors find this edition helpful in identifying and evaluating Flow Blue China.

Mary Frank Gaston
P. O. Box 342
Bryan, TX 77806

Origins of Flow Blue

"There's a joy without
canker or cork
There's a pleasure
eternally new
Tis to gloat on the glaze
and the mark
Of china that's ancient
and blue."
Andrew Lang, from the
Ballad of Blue China

These words seem an apt description for collectors of one very interesting category of antiques – Flow Blue China. "Flow Blue" is the term used to describe ceramic items (semi-porcelain, stoneware, or porcelain) which have been decorated with blue underglaze designs and have a smudged or blurred appearance rather than a sharp, clear pattern. The blue color "bleeds" or "flows" onto the white body of the piece at the time the glaze decoration is fired in the kiln.

This particular method of decorating ceramics originated with potters located in the historic Staffordshire district of England sometime in the late 1820s. According to G. Bernard Hughes (*English and Scottish Earthenwares*, n.d.), Josiah Wedgwood II invented this technique of decoration. Hughes notes that certain chemical substances of saltpetre, borax and white lead were put in the saggers during the time of the "glost" (glaze) firing to achieve a "softer texture."

England became not only the first but the largest producer of this type of ware. Other European potters decorated in this manner to some extent later in the century. Also several potteries in the United States followed the English toward the end of the nineteenth century. Examples from these other countries as well as from England are included in this book.

The history of the Staffordshire pottery industry as well as the history of pottery and porcelain making and decorating in general, and in England, specifically, are indeed of interest to the collector. However, only a brief and fleeting glimpse of this industry as it relates to our subject, "Flow Blue," can be offered here. (Please see the Terms and Explanations section for relevant terms associated with this industry and entries in the Bibliography for more detailed historical and technical information.)

"Flow Blue" was actually the consequence of two important inventions: Underglaze decoration and Transfer printing. Underglaze decoration is superior to overglaze decoration because the pattern is sealed, so to speak, and cannot be worn off through use. Handpainted underglaze decoration in blue had been used by the Chinese on porcelain for centuries. The decoration was blue because that was the one color the Chinese had discovered that would tolerate the high temperatures required to fire a glaze on a ceramic body. The color was obtained from the mineral, cobalt. Chinese blue and white decorated porcelain had been exported to England as early as the 1600s. Attempts to emulate this type of decoration were not successful, however, until the next century. When the English potters were able to obtain this cobalt color, the majority of which had to be imported from Saxony, English ceramics could also have underglaze handpainted blue decoration. Handpainted decoration was, of course, attractive and was especially desirable once such decoration could be applied under the glaze. However, handpainted designs still required a lot of time because each item had to be decorated individually.

Toward the middle of the 1700s the process of transfer printing was invented. (See the Terms and Explanations section for a definition of this process.) Transfer printing allowed the same design to be used over and over again. It was quicker and cheaper than handpainted decoration. Before underglaze decoration was possible, transfer patterns were applied over the glaze on ceramic bodies. They too, like handpainted overglaze designs, showed signs of wear and use through time. Once the technique for underglaze decoration was found to be possible by using this substance obtained from cobalt, the door was opened for decorating with blue transfer printed patterns underglaze as well as handpainted underglaze designs.

The Worcester factory is considered to be the first to accomplish underglaze transfer printing on porcelain bodies in the 1760s. Thomas Turner at the Caughley works is usually credited with being the first, circa 1780, to use transfer designs underglaze on earthenware bodies. It is important to note that it was necessity, not choice, that caused the first underglaze transfer patterns to be in blue rather than some other color. During the first quarter of the nineteenth century, blue underglaze transfer designs were firmly established as a decorating technique. By the mid 1800s, it was also possible to use colors other than blue underglaze.

The combination of underglaze decoration and transfer printing revolutionized the English ceramic industry. When these processes were perfected, ceramics could be decorated quickly, efficiently, and inexpensively. Attractive patterns with elaborate detail could be applied to all manner of tableware and accessories, making matched sets possible and also affordable for the mass population.

Flow Blue was also born as a result of these processes. The first blue underglaze transfer patterns were not Flow Blue, but Flow Blue was a direct result of these techniques. The transfer patterns had to be applied in sections on the borders and sides of objects. If the process was not done correctly, the seams where the sections were joined were quite noticeable and of course not attractive. Therefore the technique of causing the blue color to flow during the glaze firing was first used as a means of hiding such decorating faults and to thus keep the design from having such an obvious "transfer" look. Eventually, the result of this decorating technique became popular itself for this "flown" look, and manufacturers produced wares decorated in this manner for their decorative appeal. Later patterns in colors other than blue were made using the "flow" technique.

The peak years for the production of English Flow Blue were from the middle 1800s through the early 1900s. Increased industrialization of the potteries allowing mass production of wares and the refinement of the underglaze transfer printing process were, of course, primary factors for the growth of the English ceramic industry as a whole as well as for the production of Flow Blue. But perhaps just as important was the export trade with America developed by the English pottery industry. The American market was quite keen for this type of ware long after it had lost its appeal in England. It is evident from the many manufacturers' names on the back stamps of examples that not just a few, but literally hundreds of English potters produced Flow Blue. The English potters did their best to satisfy the tremendous export demand. If the demand had not been so great in America, it is highly unlikely that such a large amount of Flow Blue would have been produced.

Collecting Flow Blue

Historically, the United States has been the center for collecting Flow Blue china. Although the majority of Flow Blue was made in England, the English have not attached as much antique or collectible value to this type of ware, primarily because it was inexpensive, mass produced, and transfer decorated. It was made as utilitarian china, with most of the production exported chiefly to the American market. The same thing is true in other areas of china collecting, such as Nippon, Limoges, and R. S. Prussia. Those porcelains were also manufactured primarily for export to America, and consequently, collector interest is in this country rather than Japan, France, or Germany. Because America is a "youngster" by European and Asian standards, it has not been possible for most of us to concentrate on china collections of any great antiquity. The large availability of such nineteenth and early twentieth century imported china thus gave rise to a collectors' market in the United States for such wares, especially during the last half of the twentieth century.

Because of American collector interest, vast amounts of Flow Blue china have been culled from England to satisfy that American appetite. I noted in my first edition (1983) that an English friend, upon learning that I was writing a book on Flow Blue, remarked that she would treat her large Flow Blue platter more carefully. And today, more than 20 years later, there may be more of an appreciation in England for Flow Blue. At least English dealers and auctioneers are aware of its steady popularity because English prices for Flow Blue reflect this situation.

The unique form of decoration is the china's primary attraction for collectors. But the majority of Flow Blue is more than 100 years old and thus is a true "antique." I think that this particular age factor is also a motivation for many Flow Blue collectors, because it allows us to touch history. In addition to beauty, age, and availability, a large selection of different types of pieces, a wide range of patterns, and a host of manufacturers combine to give Flow Blue an inherent facility for collectibility.

Objects

A large number of items were a necessary part of life for people during this primarily Victorian era in history. Most of these items can be classified as table wares or personal accessories, such as dresser sets and wash sets. These pieces of china were inexpensive and intended for daily use. But many of the "necessary" items of that time are considered "rare" today, basically because of their scarcity. The pieces were used, thus they became chipped, cracked, and broken through time. So a wash basin, a toothbrush holder, or a chamber pot (especially one with a lid) are scarce today. More plates and bowls in table wares were made than serving or condiment pieces. Cheese dishes, egg holders, and tureens, for example, are rare, as are cups, which seem to be the first to go from every set of dishes! Art or decorative pieces in Flow Blue, such as vases, portrait or wall plaques, and jardinieres are also more rare than table wares, because fewer were made. Miniatures and children's dishes are other scarce categories of Flow Blue.

Not only the type of object, but the mold design and body shape of those objects are of collector interest. Look at the shape of an object without regard to its pattern or color. You will see that a plate, for instance, may be completely round in shape, or scalloped or paneled. A plate may be nearly flat or have a rather deep well. A bowl may be completely curved or have a wide outer flange. Hollow wares (cups, teapots, pitchers) may have smooth spherical shapes or definite sides. Their bases and borders may also be sided, round, or scalloped. Their handles, feet, and finials may be straight, simply curved, or elaborately formed with curved and twisted shapes. Swirled scroll designs, beaded work, or floral motifs may appear as part of the ceramic body on all types of pieces. These diverse body shapes and body decorations give the china a unique appearance and add diversity and interest to a collection. The same qualities may also indicate the particular time period when the pieces were made. Sided and plainly shaped items are considered older than those with rounded or scalloped shapes. Ornate molded body designs as well as fancy handles and finials are considered later than those more plainly designed.

Methods and Patterns of Decoration

The "flowing" look is, of course, the main point of differentiation between Flow Blue and other blue and white decorated ceramics. The "flow" may vary from very dark to quite faint. It may cover the entire surface of the piece or be confined to only the outer border. The degree of darkness of the blue is sometimes thought to be the main criterion of age, for the early blue printing was very dark. Through time, however, lighter shades of blue were perfected and desired. During the period when most of the examples we see today were made, it was possible to "flow" the patterns in various shades of blue. The lighter flown patterns are usually not as valuable as the darker ones. Some flown patterns also look more gray than blue, and the color is referred to as "slate." Purists may not consider the slate-colored pieces authentic Flow Blue, but such patterns are included in many Flow Blue collections. Value is lower than for a "true blue" example.

Transfer decoration was used as the primary method of decorating Flow Blue. Intricate borders and elaborate center patterns were possible with this method. Look closely at the various components in a border pattern. The many different designs composing the pattern often seem to defy description. However, the overall design will have a main point of characterization, details which are repeated so that it is possible to distinguish it from another pattern. Geometric, scroll, and floral shapes categorize most Flow Blue border patterns. Sometimes scenic or figural cameos are featured on the borders, often repeating the center pattern. Other examples may have only bands of color on the border.

Some pieces do not have any border pattern at all. Yet, some Flow Blue patterns have only a border pattern. But the majority of patterns are "full" patterns, with both a center and border design. The center pattern may repeat or enlarge the chief characteristic of the border, or it may be entirely different from the border design. Some manufacturers made two versions of the same pattern: one with only a border and the other with a border and a center pattern. The size and shape of pieces often determined how much of a pattern could be applied to a piece. Therefore, cups and butter pats, for instance, may have only partial patterns of their large matching counterparts such as plates and platters. In other cases, the patterns were replicated but scaled down to size to fit the piece.

The decorative themes of the transfer patterns found on Flow Blue are numerous and varied and reflect the popular artistic tastes of the times when the china was made. We know that the very first English underglaze patterns sought to emulate the Chinese designs. This Oriental influence was carried on during the early days of Flow Blue production. Later patterns depicted figural and scenic designs of a historical or romantic nature, and of course floral patterns were very popular. Animal, bird, and portrait themes are found to a lesser extent.

Sometimes other colors were added over the glaze to the Flow Blue transfer patterns. Such examples are called polychrome Flow Blue. Such pieces are quite attractive if the hand applied color has not become worn off through time or use. During the late 1800s and early 1900s, the polychrome colors could be applied with the pattern under the glaze. Other forms of pattern embellishment included gold trim or enameled work, often on the borders of the pieces.

While Flow Blue patterns were mostly applied as transfer designs, hand-painted patterns were made as well. Many of the hand-painted examples are early and were made around the mid-1800s or before. Examples are usually unmarked as to manufacturer or pattern. Popular names have evolved to identify some of these. The patterns are simple in design and usually have floral or fruit themes, such as flowers, leaves, vines, and berries. Other hand-painted Flow Blue just exhibits gradations of the flowing color on the body of an object or molded body designs painted with the deep cobalt blue. Copper lustre or other colors applied over the glaze are also seen on hand painted Flow Blue. Other colors were sometimes added to the hand-painted Flow Blue patterns. This polychrome decoration on hand-painted patterns is referred to as "Gaudy Flow Blue."

Patterns and Pattern Marks

The prolific manufacturers of Flow Blue were not content to make just a few patterns, or even just a few hundred patterns. A minimum estimate would be that over 1,500 different Flow Blue patterns were made during the relatively long period of its production. The majority of the patterns have a pattern name printed on the back or base of the object. Often these pattern marks are fancy and are quite decorative themselves. The pattern names are usually combined with the manufacturer's mark. Therefore Flow Blue collectors do have a definite advantage in identifying patterns. So many other types of European table wares from this era in time did not have pattern name marks. As a result, involved systems have been designed to classify such patterns for collectors.

Identifying Flow Blue patterns by the pattern name stamped on china is not always as straightforward as one would wish. The reason is because many companies used the same patterns. As a result, one finds examples of the same pattern with different manufacturer's marks. That is not so bad if the patterns are the same and marked with the same pattern name. But the same patterns often have entirely different names as well as different manufacturers.

Additionally some pattern names were used by many different companies, but the patterns are not the same — only the name of the pattern. Occasionally one also finds that one company gave the same pattern name to more than one design. Sometimes in these latter instances, the borders of the patterns may be the same, but the center designs are different. In some cases, the patterns are completely different. It is very likely that mistakes were made in marking the pieces with the wrong pattern name through haste or carelessness which resulted in this form of duplication.

The Staffordshire potters and other Flow Blue manufacturers did not intentionally set out to give today's collectors a headache when they duplicated Flow Blue pattern names and patterns. The basic reason for this duplication was a result of the transfer printing process. Once this procedure was perfected, engraving patterns for use on ceramics became a business itself.

Thomas Minton left the Caughley works to become a master engraver in London. He sold his patterns to various potteries as did other engravers. The purchasers could do what they pleased with the transfers. They could use the name that the pattern might have been given, or they could decide on their own name for the pattern. They could also print the pattern with or without the "flow" technique, and in colors other than blue (after it was possible to use other colors underglaze). The makers had no idea that the wares they were making and naming would eventually be of antique or historical interest. They were making the dishes for the present as quickly and cheaply as they could. It did not matter if more than one company called the same pattern the same name, or a different name, or if they called entirely different patterns the same name.

In other instances, we find that when one company took over another, the pattern names were continued although the manufacturer's mark might change. "Seville," by New Wharf Pottery and "Seville" by Wood and Son are the same pattern and were made at the same factory, but some examples have one company name and some another, because Wood and Son purchased the New Wharf Pottery. The chronology of this form of successive ownership or "changing hands" in the English pottery industry is well documented by Godden and helps to clarify some of the duplications of patterns and company marks found on Flow Blue.

In this edition, I have included more references to this type of confusion for Flow Blue patterns. For example, I have noted in the captions of a number of patterns if that particular pattern was made by another factory with the same pattern name or a different pattern name. Although this type of cross-referencing is not comprehensive, it does include some of the most commonly found duplications.

It is interesting just to browse through a list of Flow Blue pattern names, regardless of manufacturer's mark. Rivers, towns, states and countries of the world as well as proper names and terms for flowers and plants are some of the broad categories into which the pattern names may be classified. Sometimes the name relates to the picture on the face of the pieces, often it does not. Because a particular flower appears to be the main feature of a pattern, that does not necessarily mean that the pattern name is the name of that flower; likewise if the pattern name is a proper name such as Janette or Florida, that does not mean that the design features a girl or anything remotely connected with the state of Florida! Personally, I think that the persons responsible for naming the patterns probably greatly enjoyed their work in concocting names they thought might interest and thus entice buyers of the wares!

Some pieces of Flow Blue do not have a pattern name marked on them. It is sometimes believed that the early pieces were not marked because the custom of marking names of patterns on pieces had not been established. However, pattern names were regularly in use in England after 1820 when Flow Blue was first being made. The custom was in practice, but it was not a requirement. Therefore some firms evidently saw no reason to mark their products with pattern names, or were not systematic in their marking procedures, because identical pieces can be found both marked and unmarked

Marks

Manufacturer's marks found on Flow Blue are a study in themselves. It is rewarding to track down or identify the company that made a particular piece in one's possession. Why is this? Why do we almost always look at the back or base of a piece to see what mark, if any, is on it? Basically we want to know how old the piece might be. Usually we can only hope to know this from the mark on the piece. If it is marked, we can look in references on marks to see if that particular mark or company is identified, and if so when that company was in business or when that particular type of mark was used by the company. In some categories of pottery and porcelain collecting, the information we do find is rather general and thus disappointing. "Nineteenth century" for example is not really too helpful as a time period, except to designate that the piece is not new. But because of the record keeping of many producers of all types of ceramic products, this type of dating is often as close as we can come to knowing the history of a particular piece.

Flow Blue collectors are fortunate because so many pieces were marked with manufacturer's marks as well as pattern marks. Most importantly, the majority of English pottery and porcelain manufacturers has been exceedingly well documented, especially by Geoffrey Godden (*Encyclopedia of British Pottery and Porcelain Marks*, 1964) and J. P. Cushion (*Handbook of Pottery and Porcelain Marks*, 1980). Collectors of all types of English ceramics are able to date many of their pieces more precisely than just to a broad time period.

As a result of such available information, marks are the best source for dating examples of Flow Blue. They are more reliable in most instances even than the shape, color (or depth or shade of color), or theme of decoration. It is important to remember, however, that the majority of dates for these manufacturers still encompass certain time periods. If a certain mark is noted to have been used from 1840 to 1875, for example, we know that the piece was not made before 1840 or after 1875. However, we can seldom say that the piece was made in 1855 just because that date falls between those years. It should be emphasized that pieces can rarely be dated to an exact year. Some companies such as Davenport, Minton, and Wedgwood at certain periods did use various marking systems to show specific years of manufacture. The majority of companies, however, did not. For those that did, references provide keys to decipher these marks.

Caution should also be used in interpreting English registry marks. These marks are encountered on many examples of Flow Blue. References provide tables for decoding these marks, but such marks do not indicate the year that a specific piece was made. (For more about this, see "Registry Mark" in the Terms and Explanations section.)

Most of the marks on Flow Blue were made from transfer designs and applied under the glaze rather than being incised or impressed. Such printed marks could be quite elaborate containing symbols and words pertaining to the name and location of the company. Frequently marks included the specific term the manufacturer used to designate the ceramic body of his ware, such as "semi-porcelain, "stoneware," and so forth. The information in the marks also often aids in determining the time periods specific marks were used. It is important to note if marks contain such words as "Son," "Co.," "Ltd.," or more than one name or set of initials. Usually such wording reflected a change in the status of the firm, and references note the time or time period when such changes went into effect.

These underglaze marks cannot be taken off or worn off through time; thus, there is no doubt that the mark was put on at the time the piece was made. However, because of the "flowing" process, many of the underglaze marks are impossible to read, for they too became "flown." In some instances makers of pieces with illegible marks or unmarked examples can be discovered by matching the pattern and shape to other marked examples. This is not always possible though because companies used the same types of molds as well as the same patterns. But if the pattern and shape of the pieces, one marked and one unmarked, are identical, the specific company that made the unmarked piece is not usually of great importance when one is wanting to match or complete a set of a certain pattern.

Because of so many variations in Flow Blue patterns and marks, it is easy to see that as much information as possible should be given if one is trying to match a particular pattern or object. Size, shape, pattern name, and manufacturer's mark are all desirable pieces of information. Pictures of the piece and its mark are perhaps the most helpful clues of all.

Evaluating Flow Blue

Collectors have long recognized the value of Flow Blue as a "blue-chip" in the world of collectible ceramics. Flow Blue prices today are relatively stable. They do not fluctuate drastically. That is, a particular pattern does not suddenly become more popular and hence more expensive. That is not to say that price variations will not be found. One will always find prices above and below, often dramatically so, the values quoted in price guides. Auction prices often reflect this as well as the most recent venue for buying and selling Flow Blue — the Internet.

Basically four factors influence Flow Blue prices. These are age, theme of pattern, color of blue, and amount of "flow." First in value consideration is age. Generally, the older pieces of Flow Blue are the most expensive. Because of the scarcity of the older patterns from the 1830s to the 1870s, the patterns made at the end of the 1800s and beginning of the 1900s have a greater value today than they did 20 years ago.

Second, the theme of decoration influences value, but the theme of decoration is often tied to the age. Ms. Petra Williams was the first to categorize Flow Blue transfer patterns into four major categories: Oriental, Scenic, Floral, and Art Nouveau. Many of the Oriental designs are from the early period of Flow Blue production. Oriental scenic patterns are more valuable than Oriental floral patterns, but Oriental floral patterns are usually more valuable than non-Oriental scenic designs because they are often older. Non-Oriental scenic designs are usually later than Oriental scenic designs, and consequently they are not as costly. Likewise, non-Oriental scenic designs may or may not be earlier than non-Oriental floral patterns, but in general they are more valuable than the non-Oriental floral designs. Non-floral patterns which incorporate geometric, abstract, or scroll designs are usually comparable in value to the non-Oriental floral patterns because such patterns were made during the same time periods. Other miscellaneous themes, such as animals, birds, or fruit may be higher in price than floral, geometric, or scroll patterns made during the same eras.

Third, the "blue color" affects the value. The darker, deeper blues are more valuable than the lighter shades. In tandem with the depth of color in price is the fourth consideration, the amount of "flow." While it is true that the darkest blue and the deepest "flown" patterns are not all early patterns, we find that many such examples are from the mid-to-third quarter of the nineteenth century and have an Oriental scenic theme. Thus they are the most valuable. Non-Oriental scenic themes can be found in deep blue with lots of flow, but they are also found in lighter shades with less flow. Thus, the darker examples will fetch more than the lighter ones. The majority of non-Oriental floral patterns have a good, true blue color, but they are often less flown. Generally the floral patterns are later than most Oriental patterns, and thus the age and the theme combine with the less flown color to make values for such patterns lower than the Oriental scenic and floral patterns. These floral patterns are also lower than most non-Oriental scenic themes.

While these four factors are the basic influence on Flow Blue prices, there are a few other considerations which are also noteworthy. There are many patterns which are considered popular, among collectors. Such patterns have become more popular than others often because there are a great many examples available and collectors are able to assemble a nice-sized collection. Some patterns which are found infrequently may not attract buyers, even though the pattern could be considered rare. While old Oriental patterns are the most expensive, American made patterns such as La Belle and Warwick are often comparable in price, although they were made at a much later time.

American collector interest for American made Flow Blue has driven up the prices for those patterns. On the other hand, American Flow Blue which only has dark cobalt blue borders, such as pieces made by the French China Company, is much lower in price.

Value ranges are included with each pattern. For all objects except plates, the price is specific to that piece. For all plates (bread and butter, salad, and dinner), values have been listed for dinner plates, referring to a 9" to 10" plate. If for example, the piece shown is a saucer or a bread and butter plate, the value listed is for a dinner plate. If the example is a butter pat or a small bowl, I have also included the value range for a dinner plate. The approximate value of a dinner plate is basically the key to the value of other table wares in the same pattern and more useful as a guide to value for the pattern. For example, a plate with an Oriental scenic pattern made in the 1840s with a value of $200.00 – 250.00 indicates that serving pieces and other pieces of a place setting in the same pattern will likewise have a high value. A floral pattern plate made circa 1910 with a value of $75.00 – 90.00 shows that other pieces of the pattern would be in a lower price range. From the examples in this book, which span the time period of Flow Blue production and include all of the different decoration themes as well as a variety of pieces, collectors should be able to arrive at an approximate value for their patterns and pieces even though the specific item and pattern may not be illustrated.

Useful Terms and Explanations for Flow Blue

There are some basic terms that are important for collectors to know, especially beginning collectors, which are pertinent to the study and appreciation of Flow Blue. Some of these basic terms with brief definitions are explained in this section, arranged alphabetically within three categories: Ceramics, Decoration, and Marks.

Ceramics

Biscuit denotes items made of clay, earthenwares or porcelains, which have been fired only once and are unglazed.

Bisque is the same as "Biscuit" except it is almost always used to refer to unglazed hard paste porcelain rather than earthenware.

Body is the form of an object.

Bone China is a type of pottery composed of at least 50% bone ash, the calcined bones of animals. It is translucent, but is not considered true or hard paste porcelain. Bone china was invented by Josiah Spode I in the late 1700s.

Ceramic means items composed of clay and fired at high temperatures.

China popularly refers to any kind of ceramic body, such as "Flow Blue China." Its true definition means hard paste porcelain.

Crazing refers to thin lines that appear on the glazed surface of earthenwares which in turn allow the glaze to be penetrated. Crazing is caused by age and heat. It results because the body and glaze of an object were not fired at high enough temperatures to become completely vitrified.

Earthenware technically is one of the two classes of pottery. Earthenwares have a porosity of more than 50%. They are composed of various types of natural clays and fired at high temperatures. They are opaque and not vitreous, although they may be glazed as most examples are. Bricks and flower pots are examples of unglazed earthenware.

Embossed designates a slightly raised design used to decorate the body of an object. Embossed designs are formed from the clay paste of the object before the piece is ever fired.

Finial is a decoration applied to the tops or lids of ceramic items. These are made from the same materials as the body of the piece.

Fired means to bake clay-formed items at high temperatures.

Hollow ware refers to molded ceramic items that are hollow or open with a definite inside space such as pitchers and sugar bowls, etc.

Ironstone is a form of stoneware where ground iron slag has been mixed with the clay. Ironstone was patented in 1813 in England by Mason.

Mold (or Mould) is a form made in a desired shape to hold the clay paste and thus give form to the object.

Molded means to shape the body paste to give form to an object, either by hand or in a prepared mold.

Opaque is the opposite of translucent and means that you cannot see through the object.

Panelled refers to ceramic bodies which are molded with definite sides rather than being totally round and smooth in shape.

Paste is the clay composition of a ceramic body before it is fired. It more commonly refers to hard paste or soft paste porcelain.

Porcelain is technically a form of stoneware because it is fired to a state of vitrification, however porcelain is distinguished from stoneware because porcelain is translucent. The term "porcelain" is used to designate true or hard paste porcelain whose principal ingredient is kaolin, a type of clay containing hydrated aluminum silicates.

Pottery refers to objects formed from clay and fired at high temperatures. The two major categories of Pottery are earthenwares and stonewares.

Relief means raised ceramic decoration which stands out from the body of the object, shaped or applied before the object is fired.

Rococo applies to ornately shaped ceramic bodies often having fancy embossed or relief designs on the body as well.

Sagger is the ceramic box that holds the objects in the kiln during the firing process.

Scalloped is a semi-circular shape, usually referring to the outer edge of ceramic items. The term originated from the shell of a scallop.

Semi-Porcelain means any glazed earthenware pottery. It is opaque and not vitreous.

Soft Paste refers to a type of porcelain. Soft paste porcelain is fired at lower temperatures than hard paste porcelain. Originally soft paste porcelain was made in an attempt to imitate Chinese hard paste porcelain. The word "soft" refers to the temperatures used and does not describe the texture of the wares.

Spur Marks are the marks left by the clay supports that were used to separate plates and bowls during the firing process. The marks are small protrusions usually found in three places either on the back or front of the pieces.

Stilt Marks are the same as spur marks.

Stoneware technically is the second major classification of pottery. Stonewares have a porosity of less than 5% because feldspar and quartz are added to the clay mixture, and they are fired at high enough temperatures to become vitrified. This is accomplished in the first firing. Stonewares are not fired to a state of translucency, however.

Translucent is the opposite of opaque and means that you can see through the object. Translucency is the chief characteristic of porcelain.

Vitreous refers to the glass-like quality given to ceramic bodies by glazes fired on those bodies. Stonewares and porcelains are completely vitreous because the glaze and the body are fired until the body and glaze become one entity, and thus the outer glaze cannot be penetrated. Earthenwares, though, are not fired at temperatures high enough to make the body and glaze one entity. The glazes on earthenwares are vitreous, that is glass-like, but they can be penetrated. That is why the glazes on earthenwares craze.

Well means the middle part inside the rim or border of ceramic flatware such as the well of a plate.

Decoration

Chinoisiere refers to decoration emulating Chinese styles.

Cobalt is an ore found in copper, silver, or tin mines.

Cobalt Blue is a color used to decorate ceramics obtained from an oxide of the mineral, cobalt. The substance is brown in color when it is applied to the ceramic body, but the high heat during the firing process transforms the color to a deep blue.

Copper Lustre is metallic glaze made from copper which has an iridescent look.

Enameled refers to handpainted raised decoration applied over the glaze on ceramic bodies. Such decoration often outlines designs in the pattern.

Gilded means to decorate with gold.

Glaze refers to the liquid, glassy substance which is applied to ceramics to make them impervious to liquids, and also used in various colors to decorate ceramics.

Glost has the same meaning as glaze.

Monochrome means that only one color is used to decorate an object.

Motif refers to the theme of decoration of an object, such as floral.

Overglaze designates that the decoration has been applied after an object has been glazed and fired.

Polychrome means that more than one color is used to decorate an object.

Slip refers to a liquid form of clay used for decorating.

Theme applies to the dominant subject characterizing the decoration, such as scenic theme or floral theme.

Transfer Decoration means that designs or patterns have been engraved on copper plates, the grooves of the design filled with paint, after which the copper plate is heated and a soapy tissue paper is pressed into the engraved design, taken off and in turn pressed upside down on an object which has been heated and coated with varnish. After the object has dried, the paper is washed off, but the design remains-thus the design has been "transferred" from the copper plate to this object.

Underglaze designates decoration applied before an object has been glazed and fired.

Marks

"England" is found in some English marks from the last quarter of the nineteenth century, but was used on all exported wares after 1891 to comply with American tariff laws.

Garter Mark is a printed mark, round or oval in shape, used in English marks during the latter half of the nineteenth century. See "Cauldon" in the Marks section for one example.

Impressed marks are made in the form of initials or symbols and pressed into the ceramic body before it is fired. See Minton for an example.

Incised marks are cut into the ceramic body before it is fired.

Limited (LTD.) is a word or abbreviation found in many English marks after 1880.

"Made In England" is noted by most authorities to be definitely of twentieth century origin, but such a mark does not specifically date from any one year, and its use was not required; thus some examples from the same historical period may have this mark and others will not.

Overglaze describes marks placed on an object after it has been glazed. Overglaze marks are hand-painted or printed. Marks applied overglaze can be worn off or taken off.

Printed Marks refer to marks made in the form of a transfer or stamp. Such marks can be applied either over or under the glaze.

Raised means marks formed in relief and applied to the piece.

Registry Marks (RD) are marks or numbers impressed or printed on English ceramics after 1842. Diamond shaped marks were the first type used and continued until 1883. After that time the consecutive numbering system, prefaced with the initials "RD" was used. Tables to decipher such marks are found in general marks books. These registration numbers were assigned to companies in order to protect a shape or pattern design for three years. When interpreted, these letters or numbers will tell you the year that such designs were first registered, but that does not mean that your example with a certain registry mark was made on the day of the month of a certain year or even a certain year. The marks were continued after the three year period. Thus they only tell you when the company registered the design, and it is possible that they used the design before they registered it. Many designs, of course, were never registered.

"Royal" is a word used in English marks after 1850.

Staffordshire Knot refers to a bow-knot shape used to mark English ceramics during the 1880s. See "New Wharf Pottery" for an example.

"Trade Mark" is a term used in English marks primarily after the last quarter of the nineteenth century.

Underglaze refers to marks applied to ceramic bodies before they are glazed. Such marks are permanent and cannot be worn or taken off (although, of course, they can be covered over).

Introduction to Photographs

Marks

Photographs of the manufacturers' marks are presented first and are divided into two sections: English and Non-English. The marks are shown by company name. The marks for each company are primarily for those on examples in this edition. The marks are not inclusive of the total marks used by a company. Information on the dates when the British marks were used is based either on *Geoffrey Godden's Encyclopedia of British Pottery and Porcelain Marks* (1964) or on *J. P. Cushion's Handbook of Pottery and Porcelain Marks* (1980).

In some instances, the precise marks on the pieces were not shown in reference books, but beginning and closing dates for the firms were noted. That tells us that a particular mark would not have been used before or after those dates. It is also very important to note that marks could change in appearance only slightly by using "Son," "Ltd.," and so forth. I have followed such small variations in dating the specific marks shown.

Many of the English marks have pattern names either inside the mark or adjacent to the mark. Disregard the pattern name when looking at the photos of the marks. For example, I illustrate over 30 patterns on pieces made by Grindley, but I show only five different Grindley marks, not the 30 separate marks with individual pattern names. In the photographs of pieces with Grindley patterns, I refer you to one of the five marks which happen to have pattern names of either Marechal Neil, Marguerite, The Marquis, Beauty Roses, or Bisely.

In the English marks section, several marks containing various initials remain unidentified. These are arranged in alphabetical order by first initial together with the identified companies. Some unidentified symbols are also shown at the end of the English marks section. Non-English marks, including U. S. manufacturers are shown after the English marks. The Non-English marks are arranged alphabetically by country of origin and within country, alphabetically, by manufacturer.

The numbering of the marks is consecutive and includes both English and non-English marks as in my previous books. In my *Second Series*, small letters were added in instances where new marks were inserted for a particular factory. In cases where a new company was being introduced in the marks section, and the company came between two previous alphabetical entries, the new company was assigned a number with the addition of a capital letter. This practice has been continued in this edition.

In the captions for the marks, I have included a brief description of the mark, using terms such as Cartouche, Coat of Arms, Crown, Drape, Garter, and Ribbon. The dates listed with a mark are generally for the time the particular mark on a Flow Blue example was in use. In some cases, those dates coincide with the beginning and closing dates of a factory.

At the end of each company's marks, I have listed the various Flow Blue patterns made by that company. The only patterns listed are the ones shown in this edition.

Patterns

Following the photographs and information on company marks, the Flow Blue patterns are arranged alphabetically. The patterns include both English and non-English patterns, polychrome patterns, and hand-painted or brush stroke patterns. This arrangement differs from my earlier books where the English and non-English examples as well as the hand-painted pieces were presented separately.

The captions of the photographs include the pattern name, manufacturer's mark number, circa dates for the marks, and value range. Unmarked examples are noted as being unmarked, and some marks are described if a photo of the mark was not available. A few examples have the notation of being similar to a particular mark. Some of the patterns are referenced to one of Petra Williams' or Jeffrey Snyder's books on Flow Blue. When an unmarked pattern appeared to match an identified pattern in one of those volumes, the pattern name was used. In some cases, these names were popular names, or names assigned by Ms. Williams, rather than factory pattern names. Popular names are shown in quotation marks. A number of unmarked patterns are also identified by obvious names, such as "fish" or "turkey."

There remains, however, a number of Flow Blue patterns which are unidentified, either by a documented factory pattern name or a popular name. Many of these are exceptionally fine examples of Flow Blue. The unidentified patterns span the entire period of Flow Blue production, but many reflect signs of being made during the early part of the era. Unidentified patterns are also found on unique or rare objects, such as a perfume bottle shown in this edition. Not to include unidentified patterns would mean omitting some very beautiful and interesting pieces of Flow Blue China. In my prior books, I showed more than 100 unidentified Flow Blue patterns. A few of them have since been identified with a pattern name and have been shifted to the "identified" category. The other unidentified patterns from those books have been omitted. All of the unidentified patterns shown here are exclusive to this edition, and are shown after the Flow Blue patterns which have documented or popular pattern names. Unidentified patterns having a manufacturer's mark are presented first in alphabetical order by company name. Those patterns are followed by pieces completely unmarked, that is, they had neither a pattern name nor a company name.

English Manufacturers' Marks and Patterns

William Adams & Sons, Marks circa 1819 – 1864

1. Eagle and Garter, W. Adams & Sons.

2. Urn and Scroll, W. Adams & Sons.

William Adams, Mark circa mid-1800s

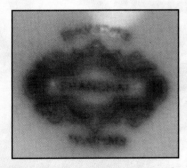

2a. Cartouche, Ironstone, W. Adams.

William Adams & Co., Marks circa 1891 – 1917

3. Crown and Garter, Crown Semi-Porcelain, W. Adams & Co., England.

4. Temple and Banner, W. Adams & Co., England.

5. Cartouche and Crown, W. Adams & Co., England, Stone China.

6. Cartouche and Crown, variation of Mark 5.

7. Crown and Garter, W. Adams & Co., England.

7a. Eagle and Cartouche, W. Adams & Co.

7b. Globe, W. Adams & Co., Tunstall, England.

7c. Crown and Scrolled Banner, W. Adams & Co., England.

7d. Eagle and Wreath, W. Adams & Co., England.

William Adams & Co., Marks after 1896 – 1914

8. Cartouche, W. Adams & Co., Tunstall, England.

9. Crown and Cartouche, W. Adams & Co., Tunstall, England.

Patterns by William Adams: Amoy, Arcadia, Berlin Groups, Fairy Villas, Fern, Garland, Gloria, Jeddo, Kyber, Mazara, Poppy, Shanghai, Shell, Tonquin

William & Thomas Adams, Marks circa 1866 – 1892

10. Scrolled Banner, W. & T. Adams, Ltd.

10a. Cartouche, W. & T. Adams, Tunstall.

Patterns by William & Thomas Adams: Asiatic Pheasants, Shanghai

Adderleys Ltd., Mark circa 1906 – 1926

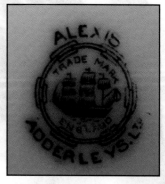

10A. Ship in Circle, Adderleys, Ltd., Trade Mark, England.

Patterns by Adderleys: Alexis, Lily

Henry Alcock & Co., Mark circa 1891 – 1900

11. Crown and Shield, Henry Alcock & Co. England, Semi-Porcelain.

Henry Alcock & Co., Mark circa 1910 – 1935

11a. Cartouche, Henry Alcock & Co., Stoke-on-Trent, England.

Patterns by Henry Alcock: Bouquet, Clarendon, Delamere, Manhattan, Old Castles, Touraine

John Alcock,
Mark circa 1853 – 1861

11A. Ellipse, John Alcock, Cobridge.

Pattern by John Alcock: Celeste

John & George Alcock,
Marks circa 1839 – 1846

 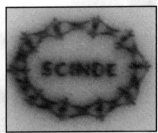

12. Ellipse, J. & G. Alcock, Cobridge.

13. Diamond Ellipse with pattern name and impressed initials and Oriental Stone.

Patterns by John & George Alcock: Carlton, Circassia, Scinde

Samuel Alcock,
Marks circa 1830 – 1859

14. Oriental Figure with Banner, S. A. & Co.

14a. Cartouche, S. A. initials.

Patterns by Samuel Alcock: Kremlin, Oriental

Charles Allerton & Sons,
Mark circa 1891 – 1912

15. Crown, Charles Allerton & Sons, England.

Allertons Mark circa 1903 – 1912

16. Crown and Banner, Allertons, England.

Patterns by Charles Allerton: Dahlia, Mabel, Wheel

G. L. Ashworth,
Mark circa 1862 – 1880

17. Impressed Crown, Ashworth.

17a. Crown & Drape, Patent Ironstone China. G. L. Ashworth continued the marks of the Charles James Mason Company circa 1862. The mark shown here does not incorporate "Ashworth" or "England," as later Ashworth marks did (see Godden Marks 143 – 145). Thus Mark 17a should be circa 1862.

21

G. L. Ashworth & Bros., Marks circa 1862 – 1890

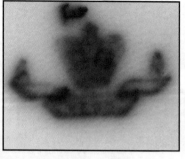

18. Crown and Banner, A. Bros.

19. Lion and Scroll, G. L. A. Bros.

Patterns by G. L. Ashworth: Hizen, Iris, Nankin Jar, Vista, Yedo

Barker & Kent, Mark circa 1898 – 1941

19A. Globe, B. & K. initials.

Pattern by Barker & Kent: Clematis

Frank Beardmore, Mark circa 1903 – 1914

19B. Bird with Branch, Frank Beardmore & Co., Fenton.

Pattern by Frank Beardmore: Dunkeld

Bishop & Stonier, Mark circa 1891 – 1936

20. Phoenix, Bisto, England.

Bishop & Stonier, Marks circa 1891 – 1910

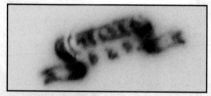

20a. Ribbon, B. & S. initials.

20b. Variation of Mark 20a.

Patterns by Bishop & Stonier: Anemone, Chelsea, Greville, Khan, Lancaster, Lincoln, Pembroke, Trent, Venice

T. R. Boote, Mark circa 1842 – 1890

20A. Cartouche, T. & R. B. initials.

Pattern by T. & R. Boote: Shapoo

Booths, Mark circa 1891 – 1906

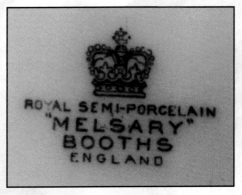

20B. Crown, Royal Semi-Porcelain, Booths, England.

Booths, Mark circa 1906 and after

20Ba. Crown, Booths Silicone China, England.

Patterns by Booths: Melsary, Simplex Pattern

Bourne & Leigh, Mark circa 1892 – 1939

21. Crown and Garter, E. Bourne
& J. E. Leigh, Burslem, England.

Bourne & Leigh, Mark circa 1912 – 1941

22. Shield, E. B. & J. E. L., Albion Pottery.

Patterns by Bourne & Leigh: Chinese, Florentine, Kew

Sampson Bridgwood & Son, Mark circa early 1900s

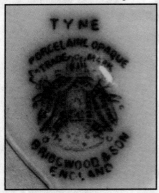

22A. Shield, Bridgwood & Son,
England, Porcelain Opaque.

Pattern by Bridgwood: Tyne

British Ware, unidentified manufacturer, circa early 1900s

22B. British Ware with pattern name.

Pattern with British Ware mark: Ivanhoe

Brown-Westhead Moore & Co., Mark circa 1886 – 1887

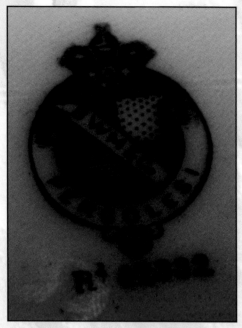

23. Crown and Garter, B-W. M. & Co., Registry Number for 1886 – 1887.

Brown-Westhead, Moore & Co., Mark circa 1895 – 1904

23a. Variation of Mark 23, Cauldon, England.

Patterns by Brown-Westhead, Moore & Co:
Breadlebane, Messina, Nankin, Pergolesi

Burgess & Leigh, Mark circa 1889 – 1919

24. Middleport Pottery and pattern name.

Burgess & Leigh, Marks circa 1891 – 1919

25. Eagle and Cartouche, Burgess & Leigh, England, Middleport Pottery.

26. Ellipse, B. & L., England.

27. Globe, Burgess & Leigh, Middleport Pottery, Burslem, Semi-Porcelain, England, Registry Number circa 1903.

27a. Globe, Burgess & Leigh, Burslem, England, Burleigh Ware, circa 1906 – 1912.

27b. Variation of Mark 27 with a Registry Number circa 1912.

Patterns by Burgess & Leigh: Apsley Plants, Burleigh, Celeste, Daisy, Eaton, Florian, Flourette, Hamilton, Non Pareil, Raleigh, Stratford, Vermont, Windflower

C. & H., unidentified manufacturer, mark after 1891

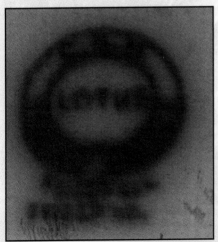

28. Garter, C. & H., Tunstall, England.

Pattern by C. & H.: Lotus

Cauldon Ltd., Marks circa 1905 – 1920

29. Double Ellipse and Ribbon, Cauldon, England.

29a. Variation of Mark 29 with a Crown, Stone Ware, Cauldon.

Patterns by Cauldon: Bentick, Candia, Turkey/Wild Turkey, York

Edward Challinor, Marks 1842 – 1867

30. Cartouche, E. Challinor, Ironstone.

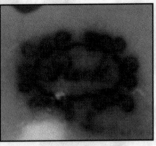

30a. Scrolled Ellipse, E. C. initials.

E. Challinor & Co., Mark circa 1853 – 1860

30b. Cartouche with pattern name.

Patterns by E. Challinor: Dahlia, Kin Shan, Pelew, Rock, Shell

Edward Clarke,
Mark circa 1877 – 1887

31. Royal Semi-Porcelain, England.

Pattern by Clarke: Lucania

Joseph Clementson,
Mark circa 1840 – 1864

31A. Eagle, J. Clementson, Ironstone.

Patterns by J. Clementson: Aster & Grapeshot, Chusan, Leipsic

Clementson & Young,
Mark circa 1845 – 1847

32. Temple and Cartouche, Clementson & Young.

Patterns by Clementson & Young: Columbia, Tonquin

Alfred Colley & Co. Ltd.,
Marks 1909 – 1914

33. Crown, Alfred Colley Ltd., Tunstall, Royal Semi-Porcelain.

33a. Variation of Mark 33.

Patterns by Alfred Colley: Lusitania, Roslyn

Charles Collinson & Co.,
Mark circa 1851 – 1873

33A. Royal Arms, C. Collinson and Co., Burslem, Imperial Ironstone China

Patterns by Collinson: Chusan and the unidentified floral pattern in Plate 753

W. & E. Corn,
Marks 1900 – 1904

34. Ears of Corn, W. & E. Corn, England, Porcelain Royal.

35. Crown and Circle, monogram, Porcelain Royal Art Ware, England.

36. Variation of Mark 35.

Patterns by Corn: Ayr, Dorothy, Flannel Daisy, Iris

Davenport,
Mark circa early 1800s – 1860

36A. Impressed Anchor with Davenport. This impressed mark was used in conjunction with printed marks. Numbers on either side of the anchor denote year of manufacture, but the impressed numbers are not always legible.

Davenport,
Printed Marks circa 1840s

37. Octagon shaped printed mark with pattern name and Davenport.

37a. Banner with pattern name and Davenport.

37b. Scrolled Cartouche, Davenport.

Patterns by Davenport: Amoy, Madras, Pekin

J. Dimmock & Co.,
Mark 1878 – 1904

38. Crown and Ribbon, Crown Semi-Porcelain, Cliff, England (Cliff refers to the proprietor during this period, see Godden, p. 208).

Pattern by J. Dimmock: Senator

Thomas Dimmock & Co., Marks circa 1828 – 1859

39. Temple and Cartouche, initial D, Kaolin Ware.

39a. Crown, initial D, Stone Ware.

Patterns by Thomas Dimmock: Chinese, Dagger Border, Orleans, Pekin, Rhine

Doulton & Co., Marks circa 1882 – 1890

40. Printed name and pattern name.

Doulton, Marks circa 1891 – 1902

41. Banner, Doulton, England.

41a. Cartouche, Doulton, Burslem.

42. Crescent and Crown, Doulton, Burslem, England.

43. Variation of Mark 42 without crescent.

43a. Mark 43 with an artist's mark.

Royal Doulton, Marks circa 1902 – 1930

44. Lion and Crown, Royal Doulton, England.

44a. Mark 44 with U. S. Patent June 5th, 1906.

45. Cartouche, Royal Doulton, Burslem, England.

Royal Doulton, Marks circa after 1930

46. Urn, Cartouche, and Crescent, Doulton, Made In England.

47. Lion and Crown, Royal Doulton, England, Made In England.

Patterns by Doulton and Royal Doulton: Arundel, Beverly, Buttercup, Carnation, Eccerton, Geneva, Gloire De Dijon, Iris, Jedo, Madras, Melrose, Nankin, Nankin Jar, Norbury, Oyama, Persian Spray, Poppy, Turkey, Vernon, Watteau, Willow, unidentified scenic pattern in Plate 759, unidentified floral pattern in Plate 760

E. W., unidentified manufacturer, Mark circa mid-1800s

48. Cartouche, E. W. initials.

Pattern by E. W.: Chinese Plant

Edge, Malkin & Co., Marks circa 1873 – 1903

48Aa. Variation of Mark 48A.

48A. Kangaroo, Edge, Malkin & Co., Burslem, Semi-Porcelain.

Patterns by Edge, Malkin: Genevese, Japan

John Edwards, Mark circa 1847 – 1873

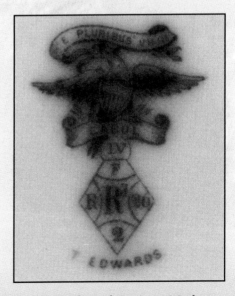

49. Eagle and Registry Mark.

Patterns by John Edwards: Cabul, Coburg

Empire Porcelain Company, Mark circa 1912 – 1928

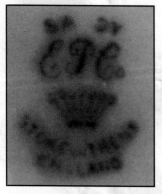

49A. Crown, script initials, E P C, Stoke-on-Trent, England.

Pattern by the Empire Porcelain Company: Savoy

F. & W., unidentified manufacturer, Mark circa mid-to-late 1800s

49B. Cartouche, F. & W.

Pattern by F. & W.: Mongolia

Thomas Fell & Co., Mark circa 1830 – 1890

50. Eagle and Cartouche, T. F. & Co. printed mark and impressed mark, Real Iron Stone.

Patterns by T. Fell: Excelsior, Japan, Wreath

Samuel Ford & Co., Mark circa 1898 – 1939

50A. Horseshoe, S. F. & Co. B. Ltd., Lincoln Pottery, England.

Patterns by Samuel Ford: Cypress, Lonsdale

Ford & Sons, Marks circa 1893 – 1907

51. Ribbon, F. & Sons, Burslem.   51a. Variation of Mark 51.

Ford & Sons Ltd., Marks circa 1908 – 1930

52. Variation of Mark 51, F. & Sons, Ltd.   52a. Variation of Mark 52, with England.

Patterns by Ford & Sons: Argyle, Bristol, Chatsworth, Devon, Douglas, Dudley, Geisha, Halford, Melton, Milan, Oxford, Richmond, Rio, Ruskin, Salisbury, Sandon, Vernon, Watford, Weir

Jacob Furnival & Co., Mark circa 1845 – 1870

53. Cartouche, J. F. & Co.

Patterns by Jacob Furnival & Co.: Chinese Sports, Shanghae

Jacob & Thomas Furnival, Mark circa 1843

53A. Scroll with pattern name, J. & T. F.

Pattern by Jacob & Thomas Furnival: Indian Jar

Thomas Furnival & Co., Mark circa 1844 – 1846

54. Scroll, T. F. & Co.

Patterns by Thomas Furnival & Co.: Indian Jar, Rhone

Thomas Furnival & Sons, Mark circa 1871 – 1890

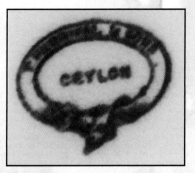

55. Garter, T. Furnival & Sons.

Patterns by Thomas Furnival & Sons: Bombay, Ceylon, Meissen, Versailles

George Grainger & Co., Mark circa after 1891

55A. Shield, G. G. & Co., Made In England.

Pattern by Grainger & Co.: Festoon

Grimwade Bros., Mark circa 1886 – 1900

56. Star in Circle, Stoke-on-Trent, England

Grimwades, Mark circa 1903 (Registry Mark)

57. Woman's Profile in Circle.

Grimwades, Mark circa 1906 and after

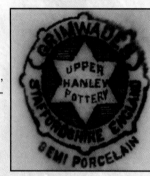

58. Variation of Mark 56, Grimwades, Staffordshire, England, Upper Hanley Pottery.

Patterns by Grimwade: Linnea, Poppea, Venice

W. H. Grindley & Co., Marks circa 1891 – 1914

59. Globe, W. H. Grindley & Co., England, Registry Number circa 1897.

60. Variation of Mark 59.

60a. Single Wreath, U. S. Patent Date 1906.

W. H. Grindley, Marks circa 1914 – 1925

61. Double Wreath, W. H. Grindley & Co.

61a. Variation of Mark 61.

Patterns by W. H. Grindley & Co.: Alaska, Albany, Aldine, Ashburton, Baltic, Beauty Roses, Belmont, Biseley, Blue Rose, Campion, Celtic, Clarence, Clover, Countess, Crescent, Denmark, Denton, Doreen, Doris, Duchess, Eileen, Florida, Gironde, Girton, Glentine, Grace, Haddon, Harley, The Hofburg, Idris, The Imperial, Janette, Keele, Le Pavot, Lorne, Lyndhurst, Marechal Neil, Marquerite, Marie, The Marquis, Melbourne, The Olympia, Osborne, Perth, Poppy, Portman, Progress, The Regal, Rose, Shanghai, Somerset, Syrian, Waverly

H. Bros., unidentified manufacturer, Mark after 1891

62. Crown and Garter, H. Bros., Tunstall, England

Pattern by H. Bros.: Petunia

Hackwood, Mark circa early to mid-1800s

62A. Scrolled Cartouche, H initial at base, see Godden pp. 298 and 299.

Pattern by Hackwood: Rhoda Gardens

Sampson Hancock, Mark circa 1858 – 1891

62B. Ribbon, S. H. initials, see Godden Mark 1927.

Sampson Hancock & Sons, Marks circa 1906 – 1912

63. Castle, Hancock & Sons, Stoke-on-Trent, England, Semi-Porcelain.

64. Crown and Ribbon, S. H. & Sons, England

64a. Crown, Opaque China, S. H. & S., England, Registry Number circa 1906.

65. Mark 64a without a Registry Number.

Patterns by Sampson Hancock: Blossom, Flaxman, Larch, Leicester, Welbeck

Joseph Heath, Mark circa 1845 – 1853

66. Cartouche, J.H. initials; also J. Heath impressed mark. This is probably a mark for Joseph Heath. Godden, p. 318, notes that there were other J. Heaths working in Staffordshire at the same time.

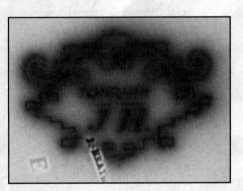

Pattern by J. Heath: Tonquin

Peter Holdcroft, Mark circa 1846 – 1852

66A. Cartouche, P. H. & Co.

Pattern by Peter Holdcroft: Chusan

Hollinshead & Kirkham, Mark circa 1900 – 1924

67. Unicorn, Hollinshead & Kirkham, Tunstall, England.

Pattern by Hollinshead & Kirkham: Alexandria

Thomas Hughes & Sons, Marks circa 1895 – 1910

68. Hughes, Longport, England

68a. Crown, Thomas Hughes & Son, England

Thomas Hughes & Son, Ltd., Mark circa 1910 – 1930

69. Cartouche, T. Hughes & Son, Ltd., England

Patterns by Thomas Hughes: Floral, Morning Glory, Regala, Shapoo

Johnson Bros., Marks circa 1900 and after

70. Crown and Ribbon, Johnson Bros., Royal Semi-Porcelain.

71. Crown, Johnson Bros., England.

72. Variation of Mark 71.

Johnson Bros., Mark circa 1913 and after

73. Square Crown, Johnson Bros., England.

Patterns by Johnson Bros.: Albany, Andorra, Argyle, Astoria, Brooklyn, Claremont, Clarence, Clayton, Coral, Del Monte, Dresdon, Eclipse, Florida, Fulton, Georgia, Holland, Jewel, Kenworth, Mongolia, Montana, Neopolitan, Normandy, Oregon, Oxford, Pansy, Peach, Pekin, Persian, Princeton, Richmond, Royston, Savoy, Stanley, Sterling, St. Louis, Tokio, Tulip, Turin, Venice, Vienna

Samuel Johnson, Ltd., Mark circa 1916 – 1931

74. Knight, S. Johnson, Ltd., Burslem, Britannia Pottery, England.

Pattern by Samuel Johnson: unidentified floral pattern in Plate 761

George Jones, Marks circa 1891 – 1907

75. Cartouche, George Jones & Sons, England.

76. Monogram and Crescent shape in blue with England, circa 1891. The smaller green mark with the words England printed above the monogram and Crescent printed below the crescent shape is circa 1924-1951, see Godden Marks 2218 and 2219. The presence of both of these marks indicates that stock originally marked during the late 1800s was re-marked at a later time.

Patterns by George Jones: Abbey, Chrysanthemum, Rebecca

Samuel Keeling & Co., Mark circa 1886 – 1891

77. Double Diamond with intials, K. & C.

Samuel Keeling & Co., Ltd., Marks circa 1912 – 1936

78. Crown, Keeling & Co., Ltd., Burslem, Made in England, Losol Ware with pattern name.

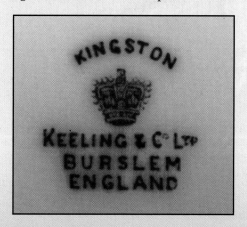

78a. Variation of Mark 78, Keeling & Co., Burslem England.

Patterns by Samuel Keeling: Cavendish, Haddon, Kingston, Two Temples II

James Kent, Mark circa 1910

79. Crown and Globe, J. Kent, England.

Pattern by James Kent: Rugge

Lockhart & Arthur, Mark circa 1855 – 1864

80. Oriental Figure, initials L. & A.

Pattern by Lockhart & Arthur: Anemone

John Maddock, Marks circa 1842 – 1855

81. Impressed mark: Castle, Maddock, Ironstone.

82. Printed scenic mark with pattern name, in addition to impressed Mark 81.

John Maddock & Sons, Mark circa 1880 – 1896

83. Crown and Circle, John Maddock & Sons, Royal Vitreous.

Patterns by John Maddock & Sons: Abbott, Beatrice, Belfort, Canton, Cimerian, Dainty, Hamilton, Hindustan, Roses & Ribbons, Roseville, Virginia

C. T. Maling & Sons, Mark circa 1908

83A. Castle, Cetem Ware, Made In England.

Patterns made by C. T. Maling & Sons: Empire, Willow

T. J. & J. Mayer,
Marks circa 1843 to mid-1850s

84. Lion, T. J. & J. Mayer, Longport, Chinese Porcelain.

85. Lion and Garter, T. J. & J. Mayer.

Patterns by T. J. & J. Mayer: Arabesque, Formosa, Grecian Scroll, Oregon

Alfred Meakin,
Mark circa 1891 – 1930

86. Crown & Ribbon, Alfred Meakin, England, Royal Semi-Porcelain.

Alfred Meakin, Ltd.,
Mark circa 1907 – 1930

87. Crown, Alfred Meakin, Ltd., England.

Patterns by Alfred Meakin: Cambridge, Devon, Harvard, Harvest, The Holland, Kelvin, Messina, Ormonde, Regent, Vane

J. & G. Meakin,
Marks circa 1890 – 1912

88. Printed name: J. & G. Meakin, Hanley, England.

89. Crown and Double Circle, J. & G. Meakin, Hanley, England, Semi-Porcelain.

J. & G. Meakin, Marks circa 1912 – 1930s

90. Crown and Cartouche, J. & G. Meakin, Hanley, England.

91. Rising Sun, J. & G. Meakin, England, Sol.

Patterns by J. & G. Meakin: Colonial, Fleur-De-Lis, Geisha, Homestead, Japan Pattern, Pagoda, Regina, Wellington, Wentworth

Charles Meigh (or Charles Meigh & Son), Mark circa 1835 – 1861

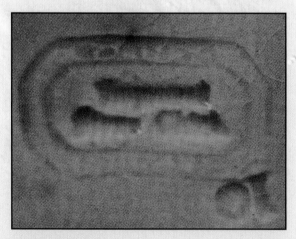

92. Impressed mark: Rectangle, Improved Stone China. Godden, pp. 428 and 429, attributes this mark to the Charles Meigh Company.

Patterns by Charles Meigh: Grasshopper & Flowers, Hong Kong

John Meir, Mark circa 1812 – 1836

93. Cartouche, I. M. initials. The first initial in the Meir mark may be either "I." or "J."

Pattern by John Meir: Chen-Si

Mellor, Venables & Co., Mark circa 1834 – 1851

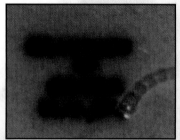

93A. Printed initials M. V. & Co. and pattern name.

Patterns by Mellor, Venables & Co.: Beauties of China, Strawberry Luster, Whampoa

Minton & Boyle, Marks circa 1836 – 1841

94. Cartouche, M. & B. with pattern name.

94a. Scolled Cartouche with pattern name and impressed B. B. New Stone.

Patterns by Minton & Boyle: Dagger Border, Mona

Minton & Co.,
Mark circa 1841 – 1873

94A. Floral and double Ellipse, M. & Co.

Patterns by Minton & Co.: Botanical, Madras

Minton & Hollins,
Mark circa 1845 – 1868

94B. Scrolled Cartouche with pattern name and M. & H.

Pattern by Minton & Hollins: Japanese

Mintons, Mark circa 1873 – 1891

95. Impressed name and Registry Mark.

Mintons, Mark circa 1890 – 1910

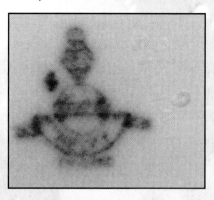

95a. Globe and Ribbon, Mintons, England.

Patterns by Mintons: Delft and the unidentified floral pattern in Plate 764

Myott, Son & Co.,
Mark circa 1900 and after

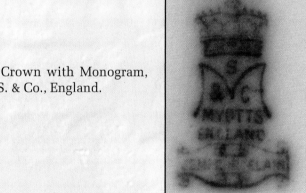

96. Crown with Monogram, M. S. & Co., England.

Myott, Son & Co.,
Mark circa 1907 and after

97. Crown, Myott, Son & Co., England, Imperial Semi-Porcelain.

Patterns by Myott, Son & Co.: Conway, Crumlin, Grosvenor, Monarch, Rose, Sefton

New Wharf Pottery Co., Marks circa 1890 – 1894

98. Crown and Staffordshire Knot, New Wharf Pottery, England, Semi-Porcelain

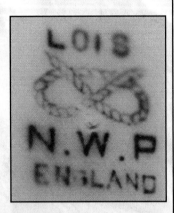

99. Staffordshire Knot, N. W. P. England.

100. Variation of Mark 98.

100a. Beehive and Urn, New Wharf Pottery, England.

Patterns by New Wharf Pottery: Astoria, Cambridge, Conway, Dunbarton, Gladys, Harwood, Kiswick, Knox, Lakewood, Lancaster, Lois, Louise, Madras, Melrose, Oriental, Paris, Plymouth, Poppy, Portsmouth, Savoy, Seville, Sydney, Trent, Waldorf, Watteau

George Phillips, Mark circa 1834 – 1848

101. Ribbon with Diamond shaped Registry Mark (for 1845), G. Phillips, Longport, Ironstone.

Patterns by George Phillips: Bejapore, Lobelia

Podmore, Walker & Co., Marks circa 1834 – 1859

102. Cartouche with Oriental designs, P. W. & Co., Ironstone.

103a. Variation of Mark 103, P. W. & Co.

103. Double Ellipse and Ribbon, Pearl Stone Ware, Wedgwood (printed in ribbon underneath mark).

Patterns made by Podmore, Walker & Co.: California, Geraneum, Kaolin, Manilla, The Temple, Warwick

Pountney & Co., Ltd., Mark circa 1900 and after

104. Double Triangle and Crossed Swords, Pountney & Co., Bristol.

Patterns by Pountney & Co.: Mandarin

F. R. Pratt & Co., Mark circa 1840s – 1850s

104A. Chinese Seal, printed mark, and impressed mark, Ironstone.

Pattern by F. R. Pratt: Shusan

T. Rathbone & Co., Marks circa 1912 – 1923

105. Swan and Ribbon, T. R. & Co., England. This mark has been reproduced (see the last section of this book on Reproductions).

Patterns by T. Rathbone: Clive, Japan, Maidstone, Norah, Princess, Trentham, unidentified floral pattern in Plate 765

Ridgway & Morley, Mark circa 1842 – 1844

106. Royal Arms, initials, R. & M.

Pattern by Ridgway & Morley: Cashmere

William Ridgway, Mark circa 1830 – 1834

107. Elongated Diamond, initials, W. R.

Patterns by William Ridgway: Penang (1), Penang (2), unidentified pattern in Plate 766

Ridgways, Mark circa 1891 – 1920

108. Beehive and Urn, Ridgways, England.

Ridgways, Mark circa 1905 – 1920

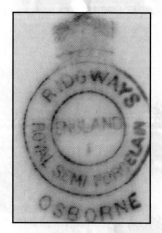

109. Crown and Circle, Ridgeways, England, Royal Semi-Porcelain.

Ridgways, Mark circa 1912 – 1920

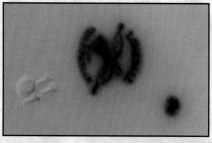

110. Bow and Quiver, Ridgways, Royal Semi-Porcelain; Bow and Quiver mark printed with Stoke-on-Trent is circa 1880 (mark not shown).

Patterns made by Ridgways: Astoria, The Bolingbroke, Chiswick, Corey Hill, Dundee, Ebor, Gainsborough, Josephine, Kendal, Lonsdale, Lugano, Olga, Oriental, Osborne, Paqueminot, Rose, Roxbury, Saskia, Sefton, Simlay, Turkey, Verona

Joseph Robinson, Mark circa 1876 – 1898

111. Flag and Ribbon, J. R. B., correction for attribution of Mark 105A in my *Second Series*. See Godden Mark 3337.

Pattern by Joseph Robinson: Cyprus

S. & E. H., unidentified manufacturer, Mark circa mid-1800s

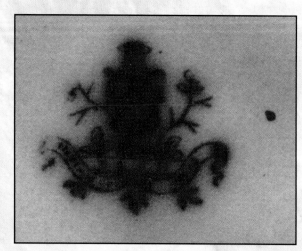

112. Flowers and Ribbon, initials, S. & E. H.

Pattern by S. & E. H.: Indian Vase

Soho Pottery, Mark circa 1901 – 1906

112A. Crown, Soho Pottery Limited, Tunstall, England, Semi-Porcelain.

Pattern by Soho Pottery: Venice

Stanley Pottery Co., Mark circa 1898

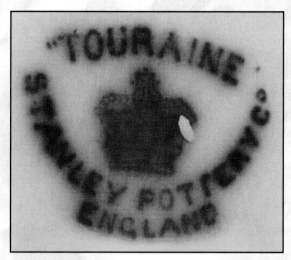

113. Crown, Stanley Pottery Co, England. This mark may be attributed to Colclough & Co., Stanley Pottery, in business between 1887 and 1928. Stanley Pottery Ltd. (1928 – 1931) continued marks of Colclough & Co. This particular mark is not shown by Godden for either company. See Godden pp. 160 and 593. Note this mark has been reproduced. See the Reproduction section in this book.

Pattern by Stanley Pottery: Touraine

Thomas Till & Sons, Mark circa 1880 – 1890

113A. Globe, Till & Sons, Burslem

Thomas Till & Sons, Mark circa 1891 – 1928

114. Similar to Mark 113A, but with England instead of Burslem.

Patterns by Thomas Till & Sons: Cecil, Nile, Venus

Upper Hanley Pottery, Mark circa 1895 – 1900

115. Crown and Circle, Upper Hanley Pottery, England, Semi-Porcelain.

Patterns by Upper Hanley Pottery: Aster, Astoria, Dahlia, Geisha, Martha, Muriel, Naida, Venice, unidentified floral pattern in Plates 767 and 768

"W," unidentified manufacturer, after 1891

116. Diamond, initial W, England

Patterns with Mark 116: Celeste, Shanghai

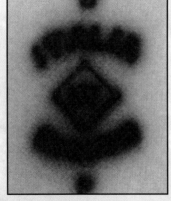

116a. Variation of Mark 116, note different style of "W."

Pattern with Mark 116a: Italia

117. Cartouche and Diamond, initial W, England.

Pattern with Mark 117: Lahore

E. Walley, Marks circa 1845-1856

118. Impressed mark, Circle and Registry Number, E. Walley.

119. Flowers and Cartouche, initial W.

Patterns by E. Walley: Cleopatra, Indian Stone

J. H. Weatherby & Sons, Mark circa 1892 and after

120. Flag, J. H. W. & Sons, Hanley, England, Semi-Porcelain.

Pattern by J. H. Weatherby: Belmont

Wedgwood & Co., Mark circa 1890 – 1900

121. Cartouche, Wedgwood & Co., England

Wedgwood & Co., Ltd., Mark circa 1900 – 1908

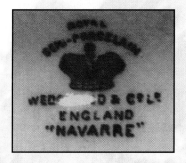

121a. Crown, Wedgwood & Co., England, Royal Semi-Porcelain

Wedgwood & Co., Ltd., Mark circa 1908 and after

122. Crown and Double Ellipse, Wedgwood & Co., Ltd., Imperial Porcelain.

Patterns by Wedgwood & Co.: Atalanta, Clytie, Corinthia, Cows, Navarre, Roma

Josiah Wedgwood, Mark circa 1840 – 1868

123. Cartouche with pattern name (impressed name with upper case letters and "Pearl" is also part of this mark but it is not visible, see Godden Mark 4086).

Josiah Wedgwood, impressed Mark after 1860

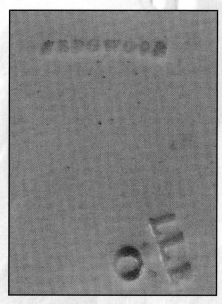

124. Impressed name with three letters indicating year. This example is for 1876 (see Godden, pp. 658 and 659).

Josiah Wedgwood, Mark after 1891

124a. Printed mark, Wedgwood, Etruria, England.

Patterns by Josiah Wedgwood: Chinese, Chusan, Ferrara, Galatea, Hollyhock, Ivanhoe, Return of the Mayflower, Turkey, Water Nymph, unidentified scrolled pattern in Plate 769

Arthur J. Wilkinson (Royal Staffordshire Pottery), Mark after 1891

125. Floral Cartouche, Royal Staffordshire Pottery, Burslem, England.

Arthur J. Wilkinson, Mark circa 1907

126. Crown, Lion, and Ribbon, Royal Staffordshire Pottery, Burslem, England.

Patterns by Arthur J. Wilkinson: Iris, Jenny Lind, Pekin, Yeddo

Wiltshaw & Robinson, Mark circa 1894 and after

127. Crown, Circle, and Bird, W. & R., Stoke-on-Trent, Carlton Ware.

Patterns by Wiltshaw & Robinson: Mandarin, Petunia, unidentified pattern in Plate 770

F. Winkle & Co., Marks circa 1890 – 1910

128. Ribbon, F. W. & Co., England

128a. Ribbon, F. Winkle & Co., England

128b. Variation of Mark 128a

F. Winkle & Co., Mark circa 1890 – 1925

129. Circle and Monogram with Colonial Pottery, Stoke England.

Patterns by F. Winkle & Co.: Agra, Kelmscott, Rudyard, Togo

Enoch Wood & Sons, Mark circa 1818 – 1846

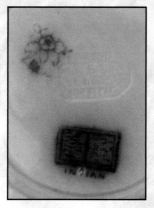

129A. Impressed mark: E. Wood, White Enamel China, Burslem and a printed Chinese seal mark with the pattern name. This is a correction for unidentified mark 133 in my *Second Series*.

Pattern by Enoch Wood & Sons: Indian

John Wedge Wood, Mark circa 1841 – 1860

130. Oval and Ribbon, J. Wedgwood, Ironstone printed on ribbon at bottom of mark.

Patterns by John Wedge Wood: Chapoo, Peruvian

Wood & Baggaley, Mark circa 1870 – 1880

130A. Crown and Cartouche, W. B. initials.

Pattern by Wood & Baggaley: Doric

Wood & Son, Marks circa 1891 – 1907

131. Crown and Ribbon, Wood & Son, England, Royal Semi-Porcelain.

132. Ribbon, Wood & Son, England.

Patterns by Wood & Son: Brunswick, Davenport, Duchess, Florence, Limoges, Madras, Manskillan, Royal, Seville, Sydney, Trilby, Verona, Victoria

Unidentified Marks

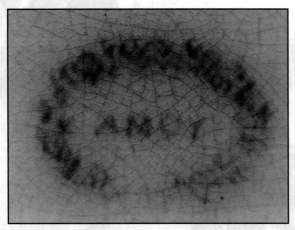

133. Scrolled Cartouche, "Amoy," pattern name, circa mid-1800s.

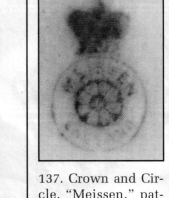

137. Crown and Circle, "Meissen," pattern name, England circa early 1900s.

138. Floral Wreath, "India," pattern name with "Amberg," printed and impressed, circa late 1800s.

133a. Willow Tree and Urn, "Ancient Ruins," pattern name, circa late 1800s.

134: Scroll and Flowers, "Chinese Pagoda," pattern name, circa mid-1800s.

139. Cartouche, "Sobraon," pattern name, circa mid-1800s.

135. Cartouche, "Lahore," pattern name, circa early 1900s.

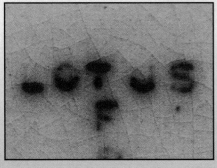

136. "Lotus," pattern name, circa late 1800s to early 1900s.

140. Cartouche, "Simlay," pattern name, circa late 1800s to early 1900s.

141. Crown, Garter, and Lion, Staffordshire, England; "Watteau," pattern name with a Registry Number circa 1910. This mark has been seen in conjuction with an impressed "British Anchor," and "Sept. 1913," which is attributed to the British Anchor Pottery Co., Ltd., see Godden p. 105. Patterns named Delft and Watteau have this mark.

143. Impressed Crown, circa late 1800s. Pattern names Delft/Delph have this mark.

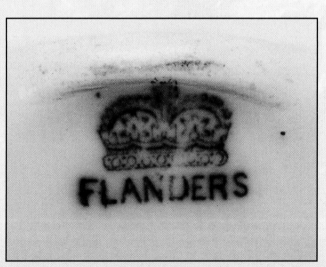

142. Crown, "Flanders," pattern name, circa early 1900s.

144. "Country Scenes," pattern name, England, circa early 1900s.

145. Keller & Guerin, Luneville, France, Floral Cartouche mark, circa late 1800s to early 1900s. Flow Blue Patterns include Eglantine and Parapette.

148. Unidentified, Crown & Shield mark, Made in Germany, possibly Utzchneider & Co., circa early 1900s. Flow Blue Pattern is Persian Moss.

149. F. A. Mehlem, Germany, impressed mark, mid-to-late 1800s. Flow Blue Pattern is Meissen.

146. Utzchneider & Co., Sarreguemines, France, Crown and Shield mark, circa mid-to-late 1800s. Flow Blue Pattern is Spinach.

150. F. A. Mehlem, Germany, printed mark, Castle with initials, after 1891. Flow Blue Pattern is Meissen.

147. "W" in diamond shape with "Quebec" as pattern name and "Germany," company not identified, after 1891. Flow Blue Pattern is Quebec.

151. Villeroy & Boch, Germany, Floral Cartouche mark, V. & B., circa mid-1800s. Flow Blue Patterns are Althea and Jardiniere.

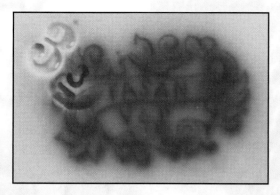

152. Villeroy & Boch, Germany, Cartouche mark, V. & B., circa mid-1800s. Flow Blue Patterns are Byronia and Fasan.

154. **Societie Ceramique**, Lion mark, Maastricht, Made in Holland, circa early 1900s. Flow Blue Pattern is Daisy.

152a. Villeroy & Boch, Eagle mark, Made in Germany, circa early 1900s. Flow Blue Pattern is Turkey.

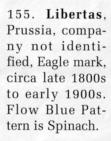

155. **Libertas**, Prussia, company not identified, Eagle mark, circa late 1800s to early 1900s. Flow Blue Pattern is Spinach.

153. **Petrus Regout**, Lion mark, Maastricht, Made in Holland, Superior, circa early 1900s. Flow Blue Patterns are Honc and Superior.

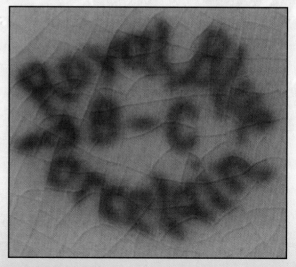

156. **Burgess & Campbell**, Trenton, New Jersey, United States, Royal Blue Porcelain, Marks 156-159 circa 1879 – 1904. The identical pattern is called, variously, Balmoral or Royal Blue.

157. Burgess & Campbell, variation of Mark 156 with Balmoral and Royal Blue.

158. Burgess & Campbell, Circle mark with Royal Blue China.

159. Burgess & Campbell, impressed Circle mark.

160. **Crescent Pottery**, Trenton, New Jersey, United States, circa early 1900s, Circle and Monogram mark. Note the Registry Mark in imitation of English marks; also this mark is very similar in style to one used by the George Jones English Factory. The Flow Blue Pattern is Utopia.

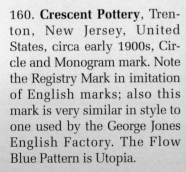

161. **The French China Co.**, Sebring, Ohio, United States, Fleur-de-Lys mark, La Francais. Marks 161 and 162 are circa 1900 – 1916. Flow Blue Patterns include Fish, Pilgrims Landing, U.S.S. Brooklyn, and U.S.S. Maine.

162. The French China Co., Ribbon mark, La Francais Porcelain.

163. **Homer Laughlin**, East Liverpool, Ohio, United States, Wings and Circle mark, circa 1890 – 1904. The Flow Blue Pattern is Colonial.

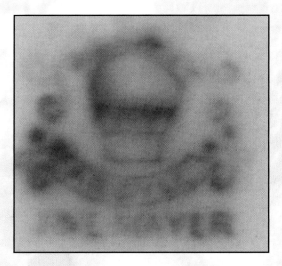

164. **J. & E. Mayer**, Beaver Falls, Pennsylvania, United States, Vase or Pot mark with Ribbon, circa 1880s. The Flow Blue Pattern is Argyle.

165. **Mellor & Co.**, Trenton, New Jersey, United States, Shield mark, circa 1894. The Flow Blue Pattern is Vernon.

166. **Mercer Pottery Co.**, Trenton, New Jersey, United States, Crown and Shield. Marks 166 and 166a are circa 1868-1930s. Flow Blue Patterns are Hawthorne, Luzerne, and Paisley.

166a. Mercer Pottery Co., Monogram mark.

167. **Warwick China Co.**, Wheeling, West Virginia, United States, circa after 1887 to early 1900s. See the patterns under "Warwick" in the alphabetical listing of patterns.

168. **Wheeling Pottery Co.**, Wheeling, West Virginia, United States, LaBelle China. Marks 168 and 169 are circa 1893. The Flow Blue Pattern is LaBelle.

169. Wheeling Pottery Co., initials, La Belle China.

170. **Willets Manufacturing Co.**, Trenton, New Jersey, United States, Globe mark, circa 1890. The Flow Blue Pattern is Ruth.

Flow Blue Patterns

PLATE 1. **Abbey**, George Jones, Mark 75, circa 1891 – 1907. Cup and Saucer, $150.00 – 175.00.

PLATE 2. **Abbott**, John Maddock, Mark 83, circa 1880 – 1896. Platter, 17", $150.00 – 175.00.

PLATE 3. **Acorn**, Furnivals, Ltd., circa 1910. Soup Plate, $60.00 – 75.00.

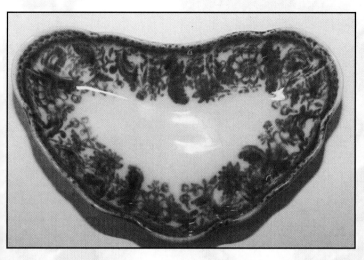

PLATE 4. **Agra** (border pattern), Mark 128a, circa 1890 – 1910. Bone Dish, $75.00 – 100.00.

PLATE 5. **Alaska**, W. H. Grindley & Co., Mark 59, circa 1891 – 1914. Platter, 12", $150.00 – 175.00.

PLATE 6. **Albany**, W.H. Grindley & Co., Mark 60, circa 1891 – 1914. Plate, $75.00 – 90.00

PLATE 7. **Albany**, Johnson Bros., Mark 70, early 1900s. Plate, $80.00 – 95.00.

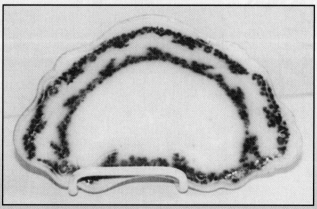

PLATE 8. **Aldine**, W. H. Grindley & Co., Mark 59, circa 1891 – 1914. Bone Dish, $50.00 – 65.00.

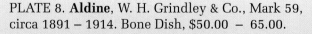

PLATE 9. **Alexandria**, Hollinshead & Kirkham, Mark 67, circa early 1900s. Soup Plate, $80.00 – 95.00.

PLATE 10. **Alexis**, Adderleys Ltd., Mark 10A, circa 1906 – 1926. Plate, $60.00 – 75.00.

PLATE 11. **Althea**, Villeroy & Boch, German, Mark 151, circa mid-to-late 1800s. Egg Stand, $1,000.00 – 1,200.00.

PLATE 12. **Amoy**, Adams, unmarked, nineteenth century. Pitcher, 7", $1,000.00 – 1,200.00.

PLATE 13. **Amoy**, Davenport, Mark 37, circa 1844. Plate, $175.00 – 200.00.

PLATE 14. Amoy, by Davenport. Sugar Bowl, $800.00 – 1,000.00 (with lid).

PLATE 15. Amoy, by Davenport. Pitcher, 5", $600.00 – 800.00.

PLATE 16. Amoy, by Davenport. Tea Pot, $1,400.00 – 1,600.00.

57

PLATE 17. **Amoy**, William Emberton & Co., marked "W. E. & Co." (see Godden Mark 1485, circa mid-1800s). Pitcher, 6", $700.00 – 900.00.

PLATE 18. **Amoy**, Mark 133, unidentified manufacturer, circa mid-1800s. Platter, 15", $600.00 – 800.00.

PLATE 19. **Ancient Ruins**, Mark 133a, unidentified manufacturer, circa late 1800s. Plate, $100.00 – 125.00.

PLATE 20. **Andorra**, Johnson Bros., Mark 73, circa 1913 and after. Soup Bowl, $75.00 – 90.00.

PLATE 21. **Anemone**, Bishop & Stonier, Mark 20a, circa 1891 – 1910. Soap Dish, $250.00 – 275.00.

PLATE 22. Anemone, Bishop & Stonier. Toothbrush Holder, $250.00 – 275.00.

PLATE 23. **Anemone**, Lockhart & Arthur, Mark 80, circa 1855 – 1864. Johnson Bros. made this pattern as Claremont in the early 1900s. Platter, 16", $500.00 – 600.00.

PLATE 24. **Apsley Plants**, Burgess & Leigh, mark is similar to 26, initials with pattern name and "England," circa 1891 – 1919, polychrome pattern. Plate, $100.00 – 125.00.

PLATE 25. **Arabesque**, T. J. & J. Mayer, Mark 84, circa 1843 – 1850s. Plate, $175.00 – 200.00.

PLATE 26. **Arcadia**, William Adams & Co., Mark 7b, circa 1891 – 1917. Plate, 10", $60.00 – 75.00.

PLATE 27. **Arcadia**, Arthur J. Wilkinson, Mark 125, circa 1907. Cup and Saucer, $100.00 – 125.00.

PLATE 28. **Argyle**, Ford & Sons, Mark 51, circa 1893 – 1907. Six-sided Tray, 9", $225.00 – 275.00.

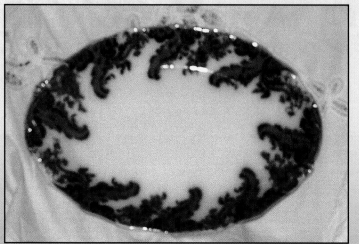

PLATE 29. **Argyle**, W. H. Grindley & Co., Mark 59, circa 1891 – 1914. Platter, 15", $250.00 – 300.00.

PLATE 30. Argyle, W. H. Grindley & Co., Mark 59. Bone Dish, $75.00 – 100.00.

PLATE 31. **Argyle**, Johnson Bros., Mark 73, circa 1913 and after. Bone Dish, $100.00 – 125.00.

PLATE 32. **Argyle**, J. & E. Mayer, American, Mark 164, circa 1880s. Pitcher 7", $500.00 – 600.00.

PLATE 33. **Arundel**, Doulton, Mark 43, circa 1891 – 1902. Salad Bowl with silver rim, $250.00 – 300.00.

PLATE 34. **Ashburton,** W. H. Grindley & Co., Mark 59, circa 1891 – 1914. Demitasse Cup, $70.00 – 85.00.

PLATE 35. Ashburton by Grindley. Platter, 16", $250.00 – 300.00.

PLATE 36. Ashburton by Grindley. Covered Butter Dish, $300.00 – 400.00. Covered Serving Dish, $300.00 – 350.00.

PLATE 37. Ashburton by Grindley. Platter, 14", $175.00 – 225.00. Relish Dish, $65.00 – 80.00.

PLATE 38. Ashburton by Grindley. Creamer, $150.00 – 175.00. Covered Sugar Bowl, $175.00 – 225.00.

PLATE 39. **Asiatic Pheasants**, W. & T. Adams, Mark 10, circa 1866 – 1892. Plate, $150.00 – 175.00.

PLATE 40. **Aster**, Upper Hanley Pottery, Mark 115, circa 1895 – 1900. This pattern with gold enhancement is also called Astoria by Upper Hanley Pottery. It is also the same pattern as Hawthorne by the Mercer Pottery (American). Serving Bowl, $125.00 – 150.00.

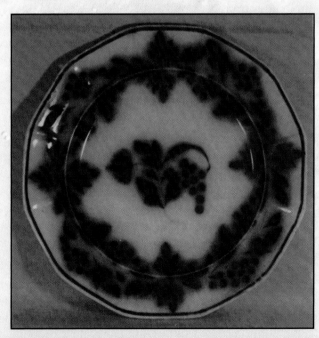

PLATE 41. "**Aster & Grapeshot**," attributed to Clementson, circa 1840s. See Williams III, p. 64. Plate, $125.00 – 150.00.

PLATE 42. **Astoria**, Johnson Bros., Mark 70, circa early 1900s. Plate, $75.00 – 90.00

PLATE 43. **Astoria**, New Wharf Pottery, Mark 98, circa 1890 – 1894. Pitcher, 7", $325.00 – 375.00.

PLATE 45. **Astoria**, Upper Hanley Pottery, Mark 115, circa 1895 – 1900. This pattern is also called Aster by Upper Hanley Pottery and called Hawthorne by Mercer Pottery (American). Serving Bowl, $140.00 – 160.00.

PLATE 44. **Astoria**, Ridgways, Mark 110, circa 1912 – 1920. Serving Bowl, $150.00 – 175.00.

PLATE 46. Astoria by Upper Hanley Pottery. Plate, $75.00 – 90.00.

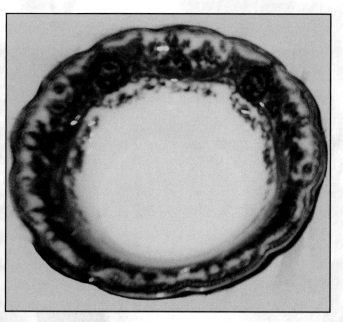

PLATE 47. **Atalanta**, Wedgwood & Co., Mark 121a, circa 1900 – 1908. Serving Bowl, $125.00 – 150.00.

PLATE 48. **Avon**, marked "Furnivals" with pattern name, circa 1890s. See Godden Mark 1651, polychrome pattern. Serving Bowl, $150.00 – 175.00.

PLATE 49. **Ayr**, W. & E. Corn, Mark 36, circa 1900 – 1904. Platter, 10", $175.00 – 225.00.

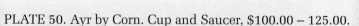

PLATE 50. Ayr by Corn. Cup and Saucer, $100.00 – 125.00.

PLATE 51. **Balmoral**, Burgess & Campbell, American, Mark 157, circa late 1800s. This is the same pattern as Royal Blue by Burgess & Campbell, Floral by T. Hughes, Roseville by John Maddock, and Senator by J. Dimmock. Plate, $75.00 – 90.00.

PLATE 52. **Baltic**, W. H. Grindley & Co., Mark 59, circa 1891 – 1914. Plate, $75.00 – 90.00.

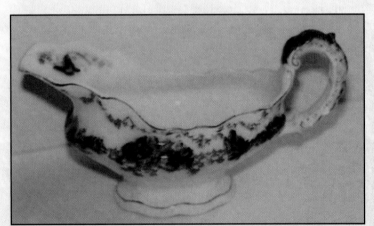

PLATE 53. **Beatrice**, John Maddock, Mark 83, circa 1880 – 1896. Gravy Boat, $100.00 – 125.00.

PLATE 54. **Beauties of China**, Mellor, Venables & Co., Mark 93A, circa 1834 – 1851. Plate, $175.00 – 200.00.

PLATE 56. **Bejapore**, George Phillips, mark similar to 101, circa 1834 – 1848. Tureen, 12" h., 15" w., $2,000.00 – 2,500.00; Platter, 18", $1,200.00 – 1,500.00; Ladle, 12", $300.00 – 400.00.

PLATE 55. **Beauty Roses**, W. H. Grindley & Co., Mark 61, circa 1914 – 1925. Plate, $50.00 – 65.00.

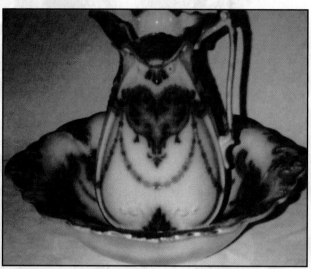

PLATE 58. **Belmont**, W. H. Grindley, Mark 59, circa 1891 – 1914. Bowl and Pitcher Set, $2,500.00 – 3,000.00.

PLATE 57. **Belfort**, John Maddock, Mark 83, circa 1880 – 1896. Covered Serving Bowl, $150.00 – 175.00.

PLATE 59. **Belmont**, Alfred Meakin, Mark 86, circa early 1900s. Covered Waste Jar, 16" h., $1,000.00 – 1,200.00.

PLATE 60. **Belmont**, J. H. Weatherby & Sons, Mark 120, circa 1892. Plate, $65.00 – 80.00.

PLATE 61. **Bentick**, Cauldon, Mark 29a, circa 1905 – 1920. Godden p. 133, notes that this factory added its name to some of the earlier John Ridgway marks, thus this example of the pattern is later than the Platter in Plate 63. Plate, $100.00 – 125.00.

PLATE 62. Polychrome version of the Bentick pattern, marked "Cauldon, England," circa 1905 – 1920. Tureen, $800.00 – 1,000.00.

PLATE 63. **Bentick**, John Ridgway. See Godden Mark 3257, circa 1830 – 1841, crown and coat of arms mark with "Stone Ware," and initials "J. R." and pattern name. Platter, 17", $1,000.00 – 1,200.00.

PLATE 65. **Beverly**, Doulton, Mark 43, circa 1891 –
1902. Soup Plate, $75.00 – 90.00.

PLATE 64. **Berlin Groups**, W. Adams & Sons,
Mark 2, circa mid-1800s. Covered Sugar Bowl,
$600.00 – 800.00, mint condition.

PLATE 67. **Blossom**, Sampson Hancock, Mark 62B, circa
1858 – 1891. Plate, $80.00 – 95.00.

PLATE 66. **Biseley**, W. H. Grindley, Mark 61a, circa
1914 – 1925. Plate, $65.00 – 80.00.

PLATE 68. Blossom, unmarked, but attributed to Sampson Hancock. Creamer, $225.00 – 275.00.

PLATE 69. Blossom by Sampson Hancock. Stilton Cheese Dish, $800.00 – 1,000.00.

PLATE 70. "Bluebell & Grapes with Cherry Border," hand-painted pattern. See Williams II, p. 216. Plate, $125.00 – 150.00.

PLATE 71. Blue Bell, unmarked, see Williams I, p. 170, circa mid-1800s. Set of three pitchers with metal hinged lids. Left, $600.00 – 800.00; middle, $1,000.00 – 1,200.00; right, $800.00 – 1,000.00.

PLATE 72. Blue Bell Covered Serving Dish, $400.00 – 500.00.

PLATE 73. **The Blue Danube**, Johnson Bros., Mark 73, circa 1913 and after. Plate, $65.00 – 80.00.

PLATE 74. **Blue Rose**, W. H. Grindley & Co., Mark 60, circa 1891 – 1914. Platter, 10", $175.00 – 225.00.

PLATE 75. **The Bolingbroke**, Ridgways, Mark 110, circa 1912 – 1920. Plate, $65.00 – 80.00.

PLATE 76. **Bombay**, Thomas Furnival & Sons. See Godden, Mark 1649, circa 1818 – 1890. Demitasse cup, $70.00 – 85.00.

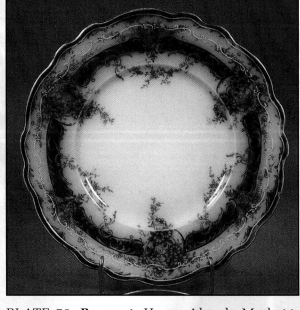

PLATE 77. **Botanical**, Minton & Co., Mark 94A, circa 1841 – 1873. Covered Toothbrush Holder, $400.00 – 500.00.

PLATE 78. **Bouquet**, Henry Alcock, Mark 11, circa 1891 – 1900. Plate, $75.00 – 90.00.

PLATE 79. **Bouquet**, marked "Furnivals, Ltd.," circa after 1913. Cuspidor, $1,200.00 – 1,500.00.

PLATE 80. **Breadlebane**, Brown-Westhead, Moore & Co., Mark 23a, circa 1895 – 1904. Creamer, $200.00 – 250.00.

PLATE 81. **Bristol**, Ford & Sons, Mark 52, circa 1893 – 1907. Bacon Platters, 9"l., $125.00 – 150.00.

PLATE 82. **Brooklyn**, Johnson Bros., Mark 70, circa 1900 and after. Plate, $75.00 – 90.00.

PLATE 83. Brooklyn by Johnson Bros. Cup and Saucer, $100.00 – 125.00.

PLATE 84. Brooklyn by Johnson Bros. Creamer, $200.00 – 250.00.

PLATE 85. **Brunswick**, New Wharf Pottery, Mark 98, circa 1890 – 1894. Demitasse Cup and Saucer, and Coffee Cup and Saucer, $125.00 – 150.00 each.

PLATE 87. **Burleigh**, Burgess & Leigh, Mark 27, circa 1906 – 1912. Platter, 14", $300.00 – 400.00.

PLATE 86. **Brunswick**, Wood & Son, Mark 131, circa 1891 – 1907. Wood & Son continued New Wharf patterns. Plate, $70.00 – 85.00.

PLATE 89. **Byronia**, Villeroy & Boch, German, circa mid-1800s. Egg Stand, $1,000.00 – 1,200.00.

PLATE 88. **Buttercup**, Doulton, Mark 43, circa 1891 – 1902. Toothbrush Holder, $250.00 – 275.00.

PLATE 90. **Cabul**, John Edwards, Mark 49, circa 1847, indicated by the Registry Mark. The same pattern with the same name was made by Edward Challinor, circa 1847, see Williams II, p. 32. Serving Bowl, $300.00 – 400.00.

PLATE 91. **California**, Podmore, Walker & Co., Mark 103a with "Wedgwood" in ribbon below mark and a Registry Mark for 1849. Plate, $150.00 – 175.00.

PLATE 92. California, Tea Pot, unmarked, except for a Registry Mark of April 2, 1849, also attributed to Podmore, Walker & Co. $1,000.00 – 1,200.00.

PLATE 93. **Cambridge** by A. Meakin, Mark 86, circa early 1900s. Soup Bowl, $75.00 – 90.00.

PLATE 94. Cambridge by A. Meakin. Relish Dish, $100.00 – 125.00.

PLATE 95. **Cambridge**, New Wharf Pottery, Mark 98, circa 1890 – 1894. Platter, 14", $250.00 – 300.00.

PLATE 96. **Campion**, W. H. Grindley & Co., Mark 59, circa 1891 – 1914. Mustache Cup, $200.00 – 225.00.

PLATE 97. Campion by Grindley. Bowl and Pitcher Set, $2,000.00 – 2,500.00.

PLATE 98. Campion Covered Chamber Pot to Wash Set. $400.00 – 500.00.

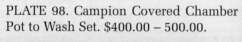

PLATE 99. Campion Waste Jar to Wash Set. $600.00 – 800.00 (with lid).

PLATE 100. **Candia**, Cauldon, Mark 29, circa 1905 – 1920. Soup Plate, $80.00 – 95.00.

PLATE 101. **Canton**, John Maddock, Mark 81, circa 1842 – 1855. Demitasse Cup, $100.00 – 125.00.

PLATE 102. **Carlton**, John & George Alcock, Mark 13, circa 1839 – 1846. Tea Pot, $1,200.00 – 1,400.00.

PLATE 103. **Carnation**, Doulton, marked on base, "Royles Patent Self Pouring, Doulton's, Burslem, For J. J. Royle, Manchester, 1886," with pattern name in mark. Tea Pot, $400.00 – 500.00.

PLATE 104. **Cashmere**, Ridgway & Morley, Mark 106, circa 1842 – 1844. Plate, $175.00 – 200.00.

PLATE 105. Cashmere Tea Pot, unmarked, attributed to Ridgway & Morley. $1,400.00 – 1,600.00.

PLATE 106. **Cavendish**, Keeling & Co., Mark 78, circa 1912 – 1936. Ewer, 9" h., $500.00 – 600.00.

PLATE 108. **Celeste**, John Alcock, Mark 11A, circa 1853 – 1861. Platter, 10", $300.00 – 400.00.

PLATE 107. **Cecil**, Till & Sons, Mark 114, circa early 1900s. Plate, $75.00 – 90.00.

PLATE 110. **Celeste**, unidentified manufacturer, Mark 116. This is the same pattern as the one by Alcock, but the mark is after 1891. Waste Bowl, $225.00 – 275.00.

PLATE 109. **Celeste**, Burgess & Leigh, Mark 26, circa 1891 – 1919, polychrome pattern. Soup Plate, $125.00 – 150.00.

PLATE 112. **Celtic**, W. H. Grindley & Co., Mark 60, circa 1891 – 1914. Plate, $65.00 – 80.00.

PLATE 111. **Celestial**, John Ridgway & Co., "J. R." initials in an oval shape with crown, circa 1841. Pitcher, 7", $800.00 – 1,000.00.

PLATE 113. **Ceylon**, T. Furnival & Sons, Mark 55, circa 1871 – 1890, 15" Platter for Tureen (Plate 114).

PLATE 114. Ceylon by T. Furnival. Tureen, 12" h., 15" l., with Platter. $2,000.00 – 2,500.00 set.

PLATE 115. **Chain of States**, names of states around border with a "MW" monogram for Martha Washington. Marked "Made in England for Oran M. Shaw, Portsmith, New Hampshire" on plate; and marked "Made in England for Daniel Low & Co., Salem Mass.," on saucer, both circa early 1900s. Plate, $100.00 – 125.00. Cup and Saucer, $125.00 – 150.00.

PLATE 116. **Chapoo**, John Wedge Wood, Mark 130, circa 1841 – 1860. Handleless Cup and Saucer, $225.00 – 275.00.

PLATE 117. **Chatsworth**, Ford & Sons, Mark 51, circa 1893 – 1907. Plate, $60.00 – 75.00.

PLATE 118. **Chelsea**, Bishop & Stonier, Mark 20a, circa 1891 – 1910. Pitcher, 8", $600.00 – 700.00.

PLATE 119. **Chen Si**, J. Meir, Mark 93, circa 1830s. Plate, $200.00 – 225.00.

PLATE 120. Chen Si by J. Meir. Tea Pot, $1,400.00 – 1,600.00.

PLATE 121. **Chinese**, Bourne & Leigh, Mark 22, circa 1912. This is the same pattern as Sobraon by an unidentified manufacturer, Mark 139. Plate, $125.00 – 150.00.

PLATE 122. **Chinese**, Thomas Dimmock, Mark 39, circa 1828 – 1859. Platter, 17", $1,000.00 – 1,200.00.

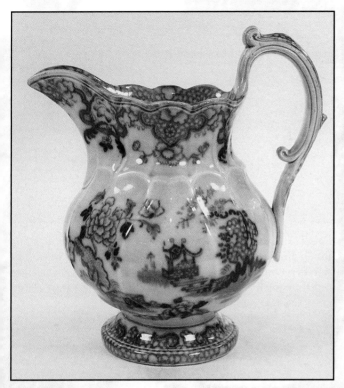

PLATE 124. **Chinese**, Josiah Wedgwood, Mark 124, impressed name, circa 1870s. Bone Dish, $200.00 – 225.00.

PLATE 123. Chinese by Dimmock. Pitcher 9", $1,000.00 – 1,200.00.

PLATE 125. **Chinese Ching**, W. Adams & Co., Mark 7d, circa early 1900s, polychrome pattern. Serving Bowl, $150.00 – 175.00.

PLATE 126. **Chinese Pagoda**, unidentified manufacturer, Mark 134, circa mid-1800s. Wash Bowl, 15", $1,400.00 – 1,600.00.

PLATE 128. **Chinese Sports**, unmarked, attributed to Jacob Furnival, circa 1850, see Williams III, p. 5. The pattern features one figure doing a hand-stand and another with cymbals dancing. Cup, $125.00 – 150.00.

PLATE 127. **Chinese Plant**, unidentified manufacturer, Mark 48, circa mid-1800s. This same pattern was made by A. S. Knight, circa mid-1840s, see Williams II, p. 239. Plate, $150.00 – 175.00.

PLATE 129. **Chiswick**, Ridgways, Mark 109, circa 1905 – 1920. Plate, $65.00 – 80.00.

PLATE 130. **Chrysanthemum**, George Jones, Mark 76 (blue and green printed marks). Vase, 16", $400.00 – 500.00.

PLATE 131. **Chusan**, J. Clementson, Mark 31A, circa 1840 – 1864. Covered Sugar Bowl, $800.00 – 1,000.00.

PLATE 132. **Chusan**, C. Collinson & Co., Mark 33A, circa 1851 – 1873. This pattern is the same as the version by Holdcroft in Plate 133. Pitcher, 11", $1,000.00 – 1,200.00.

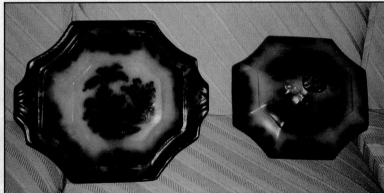

PLATE 134. Chusan, unmarked, but the pattern is the same as that by Holdcroft. Covered Serving Dish, $1,000.00 – 1,200.00.

PLATE 133. **Chusan**, Peter Holdcroft & Co., Mark 66A, circa 1846 – 1852. Plate, $175.00 – 200.00.

PLATE 136. **Chusan**, unmarked, attributed to Francis Morley & Co., circa mid-1800s, see Williams II, p. 38. Tureen, $2,000.00 – 2,500.00 with lid.

PLATE 135. Chusan Platter matching Serving Dish. $800.00 – 1,000.00.

PLATE 138. **Chusan**, unmarked except for pattern name, circa late 1800s. Cake Stand (base not visible), $500.00 – 600.00.

PLATE 137. **Chusan**, border pattern, Josiah Wedgwood, circa late 1800s. The floral center pattern on this piece is different from the one shown in Williams I, p. 21. Rectangular Dish, $200.00 – 250.00.

PLATE 140. **Circassia**, J. & G. Alcock, Mark 12, circa 1839 – 1846. Covered Serving Bowl with Pedestal Base, $1,000.00 – 1,200.00.

PLATE 139. **Cimerian**, John Maddock, Marks 81 and 82, circa 1842 – 1855. Soup Plate, $175.00 – 200.00.

PLATE 142. Claremont by Johnson Bros. Covered Serving Bowl, $300.00 – 350.00.

PLATE 141. **Claremont**, Johnson Bros., Mark 70, circa 1900 and after. The pattern is the same as Anemone by Lockhart & Arthur. Plate, $75.00 – 90.00.

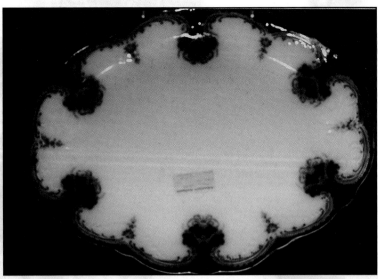

PLATE 144. **Clarence**, Johnson Bros., Mark 72, circa 1900 and after. Platter, 16", $275.00 – 325.00.

PLATE 143. **Clarence**, W. H. Grindley & Co., Mark 59, circa 1891 – 1914. Soup Bowl, $75.00 – 90.00.

PLATE 145. **Clarendon**, Henry Alcock, Mark 11, circa 1891 – 1900. Platter, 18", $300.00 – 400.00.

PLATE 146. **Clayton**, Johnson Bros., Mark 70, circa 1900 and after. Soup Bowl, $60.00 – 75.00.

PLATE 148. **Cleopatra**, E. Walley, Mark 118, circa 1845 – 1856. Fruit Compote, 9" x 13", $1,200.00 – 1,400.00.

PLATE 147. **Clematis**, Barker & Kent, Mark 19A, circa early 1900s. Vase, 8", $350.00 – 400.00.

PLATE 149. Cleopatra Cake Stand, unmarked except for the pattern name, but attributed to E. Walley. $800.00 – 1,000.00.

PLATE 150. **Clifton**, W. H. Grindley & Co., Mark 60, circa 1891 – 1914. Pitcher, 8", $400.00 – 500.00.

PLATE 152. **Clover**, W. H. Grindley & Co., Mark 59, circa 1891 – 1914. Platter, 12", $150.00 – 200.00. Pitcher, 7", $225.00 – 275.00.

PLATE 151. **Clive**, T. Rathbone & Co., Mark 105, circa 1912 – 1923. Pitcher, 8", $400.00 – 500.00.

PLATE 153. **Clytie**, Wedgwood & Co., Mark 121a, circa 1900 – 1908. Platter, 16", $700.00 – 900.00.

PLATE 154. Clytie by Wedgwood & Co. Plate, $125.00 – 150.00.

PLATE 155. **Coburg**, John Edwards, impressed initials, "J. E." with "Warranted," circa 1847 – 1873. Plate, $175.00 – 225.00.

PLATE 156. **Colonial**, Homer Laughlin, American, Mark 163, circa late 1800s. Plate, $30.00 – 40.00.

PLATE 157. Colonial by Homer Laughlin. Cup and Saucer, $35.00 – 45.00.

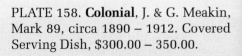

PLATE 158. **Colonial**, J. & G. Meakin, Mark 89, circa 1890 – 1912. Covered Serving Dish, $300.00 – 350.00.

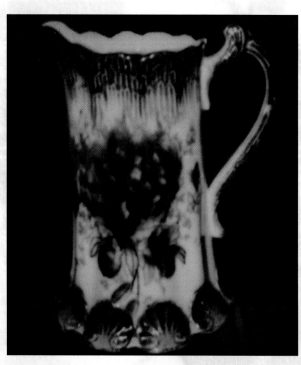

PLATE 159. **Columbia**, Clementson & Young, Mark 32, circa 1845 – 1847. Sugar Bowl, $800.00 – 1,000.00 (with lid).

PLATE 160. **Conway**, Myott, Son & Co., see Godden Mark 2809, circa 1898 – 1902. Pitcher, 7", $300.00 – 400.00.

PLATE 161. **Conway**, New Wharf Pottery, Mark 98, circa 1890 – 1894. Plate, $75.00 – 90.00.

PLATE 162. **Coral**, Johnson Bros., Mark 73, circa 1913 and after. Soup Plate, $65.00 – 80.00.

PLATE 163. Coral by Johnson Bros. Sugar Bowl, $150.00 – 200.00.

PLATE 164. **Corey Hill**, unmarked except for "Warren, Dublin." This pattern is attributed to Ridgways, circa 1880, because examples have been found with Ridgways Bow & Quiver Stoke-on-Trent mark, see Godden Mark 3310; polychrome pattern. Platter, 21", with deep well on one end and scalloped feet on the other, $1,200.00 – 1,400.00.

PLATE 165. **Corinthia**, Wedgwood & Co., Mark 121, circa 1890 – 1900. Cup and Saucer, $150.00 – 175.00.

PLATE 166. **Countess**, W. H. Grindley & Co., circa 1891 – 1914, polychrome pattern. Plate, $100.00 – 125.00.

PLATE 167. **Country Scenes**, unidentified manufacturer, Mark 144, circa early 1900s. Plate, $100.00 – 125.00.

PLATE 168. **Cows**, Wedgwood & Co., Mark 122, circa 1908 and after. Platter, 17", $1,000.00 – 1,200.00.

PLATE 169. **Crescent**, W. H. Grindley & Co., Mark 59, circa 1891 – 1914. Soup Plate with gold lustre designs added to the pattern, $75.00 – 90.00.

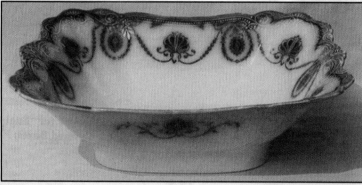

PLATE 171. Crescent Serving Bowl, $150.00 – 175.00.

PLATE 170. Crescent Cake Plate, $150.00 – 175.00.

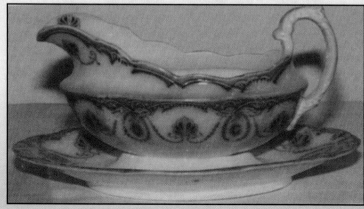

PLATE 172. Crescent Gravy Dish, $175.00 – 225.00 set.

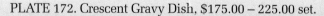

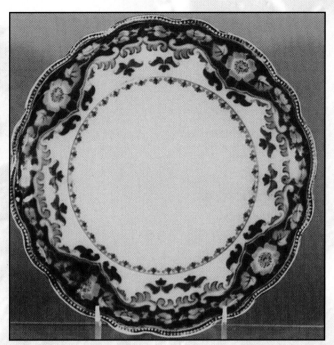

PLATE 173. Crescent Soup Tureen, 7" x 14", $600.00 – 700.00.

PLATE 174. **Crumlin**, Myott, Son & Co., Mark 96, circa 1900 and after. Soup Plate, $70.00 – 85.00.

PLATE 175. Crumlin Pitcher, 10", $500.00 – 600.00.

PLATE 176. Crumlin Covered Serving Dish, unmarked, attributed to Myott. $300.00 – 350.00.

PLATE 177. **Cypress**, unmarked, attributed to Samuel Ford & Co., circa early 1900s. See Snyder, 1992, p. 93. Pitcher, 8", $400.00 – 500.00.

PLATE 178. **Cyprus**, Joseph Robinson, Mark 111, circa 1876 – 1898. This is a correction for plate 96 in my *Second Series* where the manufacturer was identified as John Ridgway, Bates & Co. See Godden Mark 3337, which is like my mark 111 on this piece. Serving Bowl, $150.00 – 175.00.

PLATE 179. **Dagger Border**, unmarked, attributed to Thomas Dimmock, circa 1844, see Williams II, p. 39. Cake Plate, $400.00 – 500.00.

PLATE 180. **Dagger Border**, Minton & Boyle, Mark 94, circa 1836 – 1841, Gravy Boat, $250.00 – 275.00.

PLATE 181. "**Dahlia**," hand-painted pattern with copper lustre, Charles Allerton & Sons, Mark 15, circa 1891 – 1912. Cup and Saucer, $125.00 – 150.00.

PLATE 182. "Dahlia" by Charles Allerton, unmarked. Soup Bowl, $125.00 – 150.00.

PLATE 183. "Dahlia" by Charles Allerton, unmarked. Waste Bowl, $250.00 – 275.00.

PLATE 184. **Dahlia**, Edward Challinor, "E. C." initials, see Mark 30a, circa 1842 – 1867. Platter, 11", $300.00 – 350.00.

PLATE 186. **Dahlia**, Upper Hanley Pottery, Mark 115, circa 1895 – 1900, see Williams I, p. 96. Serving Bowl, $150.00 – 175.00.

PLATE 185. Dahlia by E. Challinor. Sugar Bowl, $600.00 – 700.00 (with lid).

PLATE 187. **Dainty**, John Maddock, Mark 83, circa 1880 – 1896. Platter, 14", $250.00 – 300.00.

PLATE 188. **Daisy**, Burgess & Leigh, similar to Mark 27 with a Registry Mark for 1896. Butter Pat, $30.00 – 35.00. Plate (not shown), $60.00 – 75.00.

PLATE 189. **"Daisy,"** hand-painted pattern, Societie Ceramique, Holland, Mark 154, circa early 1900s, see Williams II, p. 218. Soup Bowl, $100.00 – 125.00.

PLATE 190. **Davenport**, Wood & Son, Mark 131, circa 1891 – 1907. Small Bowl, $25.00 – 35.00. Plate (not shown), $65.00 – 80.00.

PLATE 191. **Del Monte**, Johnson Bros., Mark 72, circa 1900 and after. Platter, 14", $275.00 – 325.00.

PLATE 192. **Delamere**, Henry Alcock, similar to Mark 11, circa 1891 – 1900. Soup Bowl, $75.00 – 90.00.

PLATE 193. **Delft**, Mintons, Mark 95 (Mark 95a is also found on this Mintons pattern), circa 1873 – 1891. Oyster Plate, $300.00 – 350.00.

PLATE 194. **Delft** or **Delph**. This floral example is marked only with an embossed crown, Mark 143, circa late 1800s. The pattern is very similar to Delft by Mintons, Delph by Wood & Son (Williams I, p. 175), Madras by Upper Hanley Pottery (Williams II, p. 257), and Rugge by J. Kent. Plate, $80.00 – 95.00.

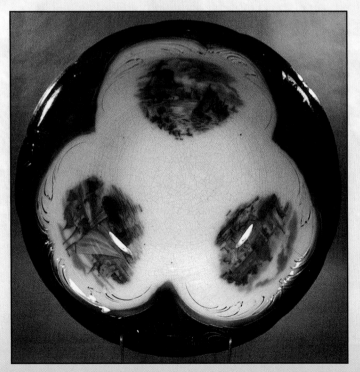

PLATE 195. **Delph**, marked "The Sebring," Sebring Pottery Co., American, circa early 1900s. Wash Bowl, 17", $800.00 – 1,000.00.

PLATE 196. **Denmark**, W. H. Grindley & Co., Mark 59, circa 1891 – 1914. Soup Plate, $50.00 – 60.00.

PLATE 198. **Devon**, Ford & Sons, Ltd., Mark 52, circa early 1900s. Covered Serving Dish and Tray, $600.00 – 700.00 set.

PLATE 197. **Denton**, W. H. Grindley & Co., Mark 59, circa 1891 – 1914. Plate, $70.00 – 85.00.

PLATE 200. Devon by A. Meakin. Sugar Bowl, $175.00 – 225.00.

PLATE 199. **Devon**, Alfred Meakin, Mark 87, circa early 1900s. Platter, 14", $250.00 – 300.00.

PLATE 201. **Doreen**, W. H. Grindley & Co., Mark 60, circa 1891– 1914. Toothbrush Holder, $250.00 – 275.00; Pitcher, $400.00 – 500.00; Covered Soap Dish, $250.00 – 275.00; Shaving Mug, $200.00 – 225.00.

PLATE 202. Doreen Bowl and Pitcher Set, $2,000.00 – 2,500.00.

PLATE 203. Doreen Waste Jar, $1,000.00 – 1,200.00.

PLATE 205. **Doris**, W. H. Grindley & Co., Mark 59, circa 1891 – 1914. Platter, 16", $200.00 – 250.00.

PLATE 204. **Doric**, Wood & Baggaley, Mark 130A, circa 1870 – 1880. Plate, $75.00 – 90.00.

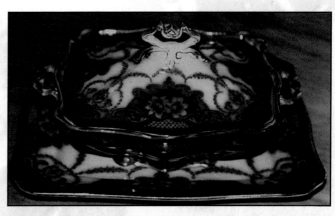

PLATE 207. **Douglas**, Ford & Sons, Mark 51, circa 1893 – 1907. Covered Serving Dish and Tray, $700.00 – 800.00 set.

PLATE 206. **Dorothy**, W. & E. Corn, Mark 34, circa 1900 – 1904. Waste Bowl, $100.00 – 125.00.

PLATE 209. **Dresdon**, Johnson Bros., Mark 70, circa 1900 and after. Platter, 12", $150.00 – 200.00.

PLATE 208. Douglas by Ford & Sons. Set of four Platters: 12", $200.00 – 250.00; 14", $250.00 – 300.00; 16", $300.00 – 350.00; 18", $350.00 – 400.00.

PLATE 210. **Duchess**, W. H. Grindley & Co., Mark 59, circa 1891 – 1914. Plate, $50.00 – 65.00.

PLATE 211. **Duchess**, Wood & Sons, Mark 131, circa 1891 – 1907. Wash Bowl, 17", $1,000.00 – 1,200.00.

PLATE 213. **Dunbarton**, New Wharf Pottery, Mark 98, circa 1890 – 1894. Bone Dish, $70.00 – 85.00.

PLATE 212. **Dudley**, Ford & Sons, Mark 51, circa 1893 – 1907. Plate, $75.00 – 90.00.

PLATE 214. **Dundee**, Ridgways, Mark 110, circa 1912 – 1920. Creamer, $200.00 – 250.00.

PLATE 215. **Dunkeld**, Frank Beardmore & Co., Mark 19B, circa 1903 – 1914. Plate, $60.00 – 75.00.

PLATE 216. **Eastern Plants**, Wood & Brownfield, marked "W. & B., Cobridge," circa 1838 – 1850. Platter, 19", $1,000.00 – 1,200.00.

PLATE 217. **Eaton**, Burgess & Leigh, Mark 27 with a Registry Mark for 1902. Plate, $70.00 – 85.00.

PLATE 218. **Eaton**, T. Rathbone & Co., circa 1912 – 1923. Gravy Boat, $120.00 – 145.00.

PLATE 219. **Ebor**, Ridgways, Mark 110, circa 1912 – 1920. Creamer, $200.00 – 250.00.

PLATE 220. **Eccerton**, Royal Doulton, Mark 44, circa early 1900s. Soup Bowl, $70.00 – 85.00.

PLATE 221. **Eclipse**, Johnson Bros., Mark 70, circa early 1900s. Berry Bowl, $25.00 – 35.00; Plate (not shown), $75.00 – 90.00.

PLATE 222. Eclipse by Johnson Bros. Platter, 16", $250.00 – 300.00.

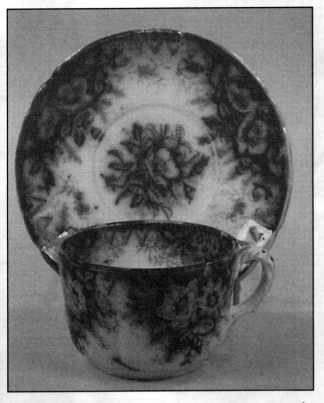

PLATE 224. **Eileen**, W. H. Grindley & Co., Mark 59, circa 1891 – 1914. Soup Plate, $60.00 – 75.00.

PLATE 223. **Eglantine**, Keller & Guerin, French, Mark 145, circa early 1900s. Cup and Saucer, $100.00 – 125.00.

PLATE 225. **Empire**, C. T. Maling & Sons, similar to Mark 83A, circa early 1900s. Platter, 11", $125.00 – 150.00.

PLATE 226. **Excelsior**, Thomas Fell, Mark 50, circa mid-1800s. Plate, $175.00 – 200.00.

PLATE 227. Excelsior by Thomas Fell. Tea Pot, $1,000.00 – 1,200.00.

PLATE 228. **Fairy Villas**, William Adams & Co., Mark 5, circa 1891 – 1917. Serving Bowl, $150.00 – 175.00.

PLATE 229. Fairy Villas, another version of the pattern by William Adams & Co., Mark 6, circa 1891 – 1917. Serving Bowl, $150.00 – 175.00.

PLATE 230. **Fasan**, Villeroy & Boch, German, Mark 152, circa mid-1800s. Plate, $175.00 – 200.00.

PLATE 231. **Feather Edge**, hand-painted, unmarked, circa mid-1800s. Platter, 16", $175.00 – 225.00.

PLATE 232. **Ferrara**, Wedgwood, Mark 124a, circa early 1900s. Pitcher, 6", $300.00 – 400.00.

PLATE 233. **Fern**, W. Adams & Co., circa early 1900s. Platter, 16", $225.00 – 275.00.

PLATE 234. "**Fern**," hand-painted pattern, unmarked, circa mid-1800s, see Williams II, p. 219. Tea Pot, $1,000.00 – 1,200.00; Creamer, $600.00 – 700.00; Sugar Bowl, $800.00 – 1,000.00; Waste Bowl, $200.00 – 250.00.

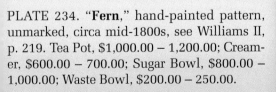

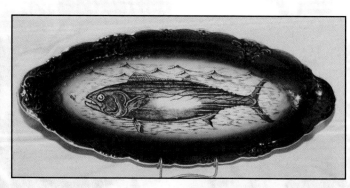

PLATE 236. **Fish**, marked "France" in green, circa after 1891. Platter, 16", $250.00 – 300.00.

PLATE 235. **Festoon**, George Grainger & Co., Mark 55A, after 1891. Platter, 16", $250.00 – 300.00.

PLATE 238. Flanders Plate, $75.00 – 90.00; Gravy Boat, $120.00 – 145.00.

PLATE 237. **Flanders**, unidentified manufacturer, Mark 142, circa early 1900s. Covered Serving Dish, $300.00 – 350.00.

PLATE 239. **Flannel Daisy**, W. & E. Corn, Mark 36, circa 1900 – 1904. Plate, $60.00 – 75.00.

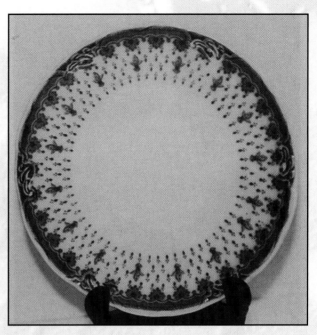

PLATE 240. **Flaxman**, Sampson Hancock, Mark 64a with Registry Mark for 1906. Platter, 16", $250.00 – 300.00.

PLATE 241. **Fleur de Lis**, J. & G. Meakin, Mark 88, circa after 1890. Plate, $60.00 – 75.00.

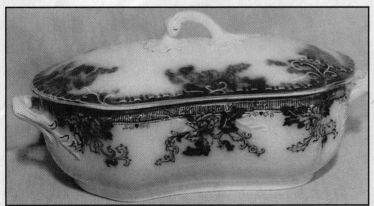

PLATE 242. **Floral**, Thomas Hughes & Sons, similar to Mark 68a without a pattern name, circa 1895 – 1910 (see Williams I, p. 178). This is the same pattern as Roseville by John Maddock, Senator by J. Dimmock, and Balmoral and Royal Blue by Burgess & Campbell (American). Covered Serving Dish, $300.00 – 350.00.

PLATE 243. **Florence**, Wood & Son, Mark 131, circa 1891 – 1907. Plate, $75.00 – 90.00.

PLATE 245. **Florian**, Burgess & Leigh, Mark 27 with a Registry Mark for 1909. Platter, 18", $275.00 – 325.00.

PLATE 244. **Florentine**, Bourne & Leigh, Mark 21, circa early 1900s. Soup Bowl, $60.00 – 75.00.

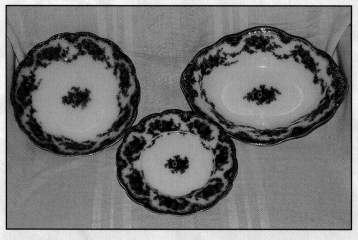

PLATE 247. Florida by Grindley. Platter, 14", $200.00 – 250.00.

PLATE 246. **Florida**, W. H. Grindley & Co., Mark 59, circa 1891 – 1914. Dinner Plate, $75.00 – 90.00; Serving Bowl, $150.00 – 175.00; Salad Plate, $60.00 – 75.00.

PLATE 248. Florida by Grindley. Charger, 15", $225.00 – 275.00.

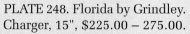

PLATE 249. **Florida**, Johnson Bros., Mark 70, circa early 1900s. Platter, 15", $250.00 – 300.00.

PLATE 250. Florida by Johnson Bros. Pitcher, 8", $300.00 – 400.00.

PLATE 251. **Flourette**, Burgess & Leigh, circa early 1900s. Egg Cup Basket, $600.00 – 800.00.

PLATE 252. **Formosa**, T. J. & J. Mayer, Mark 85, circa 1843 to mid-1850s. Serving Bowl, $300.00 – 350.00.

PLATE 253. Formosa by Mayer. Pitcher, 6",
$700.00 – 800.00.

PLATE 254. **Formosa**, William Ridgway, circa mid-1800s. This
is the same pattern as Penang by William Ridgway. Platter,
16", $1,200.00 – 1,400.00.

PLATE 255. **Fulton**, Johnson Bros., similar to Mark
71, circa early 1900s. Plate, $65.00 – 80.00.

PLATE 256. **Gainsborough**, Ridgways, Mark 109, circa 1905 –
1920. Sugar Bowl, $150.00 – 200.00.

PLATE 257. Gainsborough by Ridgways. Cheese Dish, $500.00 – 600.00.

PLATE 258. **Galatea**, Josiah Wedgwood, similar to Mark 124a, after 1891. Toothbrush Holder, $100.00 – 175.00.

PLATE 259. **Garland**, W. Adams & Co., Mark 3, circa after 1891. Chamber Pot, $300.00 – 400.00.

PLATE 260. **Geisha**, Ford & Sons, Mark 52, circa after 1908. Plate, $100.00 – 125.00.

115

PLATE 261. **Geisha**, J. & G. Meakin, Mark 88, circa after 1890. Serving Bowl, $150.00 – 175.00.

PLATE 262. **Geisha**, Upper Hanley Pottery, Mark 115, circa 1895 – 1900. Serving Bowl, $175.00 – 200.00.

PLATE 263. **Geneva**, Doulton, Mark 45, circa 1902 – 1930. Pitcher, 6", $400.00 – 500.00.

PLATE 264. **Genevese**, Edge, Malkin & Co., Mark 48A, circa 1873 – 1903. Plate, $125.00 – 150.00.

PLATE 265. Genevese by Edge, Malkin & Co., Mark 48Aa. Serving Dish, $300.00 – 350.00.

PLATE 266. **Georgia**, Johnson Bros., Mark 73, circa 1913 and after. Platter, 10", $150.00 – 200.00.

PLATE 267. **Geraneum**, Podmore, Walker & Co., similar to Mark 102, circa 1834 – 1859. Plate, $140.00 – 165.00.

PLATE 268. "**Gingham Flower**," hand-painted pattern, unmarked, circa mid-1800s. Plate, $125.00 – 150.00.

PLATE 270. Gironde Covered Butter Dish, $300.00 – 400.00.

PLATE 269. **Gironde**, W. H. Grindley & Co., Mark 59, circa 1891 – 1914. Berry Dish, $30.00 – 35.00. Plate (not shown), $70.00 – 85.00.

PLATE 272. **Gladys**, unmarked, attributed to New Wharf Pottery, circa 1890 – 1894. Waste Bowl, $150.00 – 175.00.

PLATE 271. **Girton**, W. H. Grindley & Co., Marks 59 and 60, circa 1891 – 1914. Platter, 16", $250.00 – 300.00.

PLATE 273. **Glentine**, W. H. Grindley & Co., Mark 61, circa 1914 – 1925. Plate, $60.00 – 75.00.

PLATE 275. **Glorie De Dijon**, Doulton, Mark 43, circa 1891 – 1902. Wash Bowl and Pitcher, $2,500.00 – 3,000.00; Chamber Pot, $400.00 – 500.00; Sponge Dish, $275.00 – 325.00; Toothbrush Holder, $175.00 – 200.00; Covered Soap Dish, $250.00 – 275.00.

PLATE 274. **Gloria**, W. Adams & Co., Mark 8, after 1896. Soup Plate, $65.00 – 80.00.

PLATE 276. Glorie De Dijon by Doulton. Foot Bath for Wash Set, $2,200.00 – 2,500.00.

PLATE 277. **Grace**, W. H. Grindley & Co., Mark 59, circa 1891 – 1914. Plate, $60.00 – 75.00.

PLATE 278. **Grasshopper and Flowers**, unmarked (see Williams II, p. 43, attributed to Charles Meigh, circa early 1840s), polychrome pattern. Milk Pitcher, 11", with hinged lid, $1,200.00 – 1,400.00.

PLATE 279. **Grecian Scroll**, T. J. & J. Mayer, circa mid-1800s. Pitcher, 6"; the spout is a figural bearded head, popularly called a "North Wind" head. $700.00 – 800.00.

PLATE 280. **Grecian Statue**, Brownfields Pottery, circa 1891 – 1900, see Godden Mark 670. Berry Drainer, $225.00 – 275.00.

PLATE 281. **Greville**, Bishop & Stonier, Mark 20, circa early 1900s. Plate, $65.00 – 80.00.

PLATE 282. **Grosvenor**, Myott, Son & Co., Mark 97, circa 1907 and after. Plate, $65.00 – 80.00.

PLATE 283. **Haddon**, W. H. Grindley & Co., Mark 59, circa 1891 – 1914. This same pattern is found with a "Libertas, Prussia" mark, see Mark 155. Plates 284 – 288 illustrate examples of the pattern by Grindley. Dinner Plate, $75.00 – 90.00; Luncheon Plate, $60.00 – 75.00; Salad/Dessert Plate, $40.00 – 55.00; Butter Pat, $35.00 – 45.00.

PLATE 285. Sugar Bowl, $150.00 – 200.00; Creamer, $175.00 – 225.00; Gravy Boat, $120.00 – 145.00.

PLATE 284. Demitasse Cup and Saucer, and Tea Cup and Saucer, $100.00 – 125.00 each; Soup Bowl, $75.00 – 90.00.

PLATE 286. Set of four Platters: 10", $100.00 – 150.00; 12", $150.00 – 200.00; 14", $200.00 – 250.00; 16", $250.00 – 300.00.

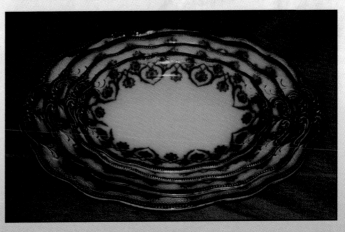

PLATE 287. Pitcher, 7½", $275.00 – 325.00.

PLATE 288. Tureen, $350.00 – 400.00.

PLATE 289. **Haddon**, Keeling & Co., marked "K. & Co., Late Mayers," circa 1886 – 1909. Jardiniere, $500.00 – 600.00.

PLATE 290. **Halford**, Ford & Sons, Ltd., Mark 52a, circa 1908 – 1930. Plate, $60.00 – 75.00; Gravy Boat, $80.00 – 100.00.

PLATE 291. **Hamilton**, Burgess & Leigh, Mark 27b, circa 1912. Sauce Tureen, Tray, and Ladle, $400.00 – 500.00.

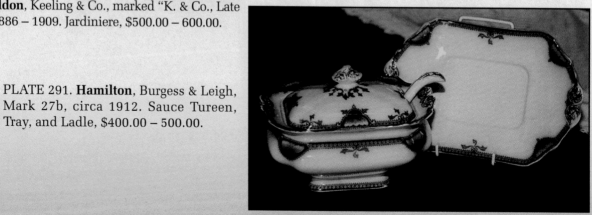

PLATE 293. **Harley**, W. H. Grindley & Co., similar to Mark 60, circa 1891 – 1914. Pitcher to a Wash Set, $1,000.00 – 1,200.00; Hot Water Pitcher, $300.00 – 400.00; Toothbrush Holder, $200.00 – 250.00.

PLATE 292. **Hamilton**, John Maddock, Mark 83, circa 1880 – 1896. Soup Plate, $65.00 – 80.00.

PLATE 294. **Harvard**, Alfred Meakin, Ltd., Mark 86, circa early 1900s. Plate, $70.00 – 85.00.

PLATE 295. **Harvest**, Alfred Meakin, Ltd., Mark 87, circa early 1900s. The pattern name is not on this example, see Williams II, p. 138. Soup Bowl, $50.00 – 65.00.

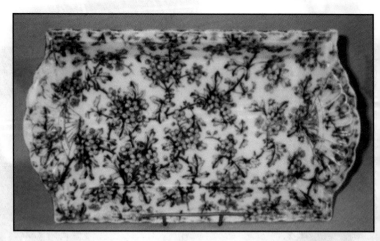

PLATE 297. **Hawthorne**, Mercer Pottery, American, Mark 166, circa late 1800s. This pattern is the same as Aster and Astoria by Upper Hanley Pottery. Tray, 12", $300.00 – 350.00.

PLATE 296. **Harwood**, New Wharf Pottery, circa 1890 – 1894. Plate, $70.00 – 85.00.

PLATE 298. **"Heath's Flower,"** hand-painted pattern, attributed to T. Heath, circa early 1830s, see Williams I, p. 182. Handleless Cup and Saucer, $200.00 – 250.00.

PLATE 299. **Hindustan**, unmarked, attributed to John Maddock, circa 1855, see Williams I, p. 27. Covered Vegetable Bowl, $1,000.00 – 1,200.00.

PLATE 301. **Hizen**, G.L. Ashworth, Mark 17 (without crown), circa 1862 – 1880. Plate, $100.00 – 125.00.

PLATE 300. Hindustan Pitcher, 13", $1,200.00 – 1,400.00.

PLATE 302. Hizen by Ashworth, Mark 17a, Chamber Pot, $400.00 – 500.00.

PLATE 303. **The Hofburg**, W. H. Grindley & Co., Mark 59, circa 1891 – 1914. Pitcher, 6", $225.00 – 275.00.

PLATE 304. The Hofburg by Grindley. Sugar Bowl, $150.00 – 200.00.

PLATE 305. **Holland**, Johnson Bros., Mark 73, circa 1913 and after. This is the same pattern as Meissen and Onion which were made by several factories. Plate, $80.00 – 95.00.

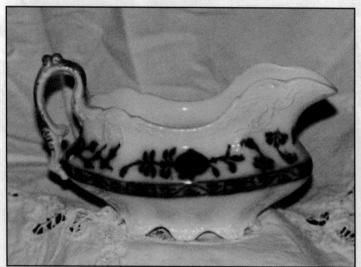

PLATE 306. Holland Gravy Boat, $120.00 – 145.00.

PLATE 307. Holland Sugar Bowl, $200.00 – 250.00.

PLATE 308. Holland Covered Serving Bowl, $300.00 – 350.00.

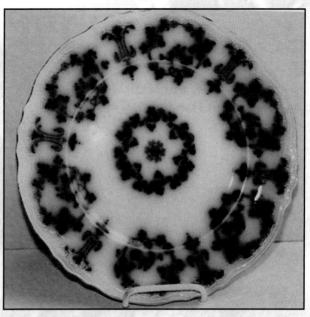

PLATE 309. **The Holland**, Alfred Meakin, Ltd., Mark 86, circa early 1900s. Plate, $65.00 – 80.00.

PLATE 310. The Holland by Alfred Meakin. Covered Serving Bowl, $275.00 – 325.00.

PLATE 311. **Hollyhock**, Josiah Wedgwood, Mark 123, circa 1840 – 1868. Plate, $75.00 – 90.00.

PLATE 312. Hollyhock by Wedgwood. Platter, 10", $150.00 – 200.00.

PLATE 313. **Homestead**, J. & G. Meakin, Mark 89, circa 1890 – 1912. Plate, $70.00 – 85.00.

PLATE 314. **Honc**, Petrus Regout, Dutch, Mark 153, circa early 1900s. Plate, $125.00 – 150.00.

PLATE 315. **Hong Kong**, Charles Meigh, Mark 92, circa 1835 – 1861. Plate, $175.00 – 200.00.

PLATE 316. Hong Kong by Meigh. Serving Bowl, $300.00 – 400.00.

PLATE 317. **Idris**, W. H. & Grindley, Mark 60a, circa early 1900s. Platter, 16", $200.00 – 250.00.

PLATE 318. **The Imperial**, W. H. Grindley, Mark 61, circa 1914 – 1925. Platter, 12", $150.00 – 200.00.

PLATE 319. **India**, unidentified manufacturer, Mark 138, circa late 1800s. Cup and Saucer, $125.00 – 150.00.

PLATE 320. **Indian**, attributed to Enoch Wood and Sons, Mark 129A. The Oriental seal mark found on this pattern, without any other mark, was noted as an "unidentified manufacturer," Mark 133, in my *Second Series*. Pieces have been found in this pattern, however, with the impressed name of "Enoch Wood, White Enamel China, Burslem" in conjunction with the printed Oriental mark and pattern name. Godden (see Mark 4248) dates that impressed mark circa 1784 – 1790. That time period actually pre-dates the discovery of and use of the Flow Blue decorating technique. It is most likely that the printed Oriental mark and Flow Blue decoration were applied to undecorated china previously made by Enoch Wood, circa the 1830s to 1840s. Plate, $200.00 – 225.00.

PLATE 321. Indian handleless Cup and Saucer, $225.00 – 275.00.

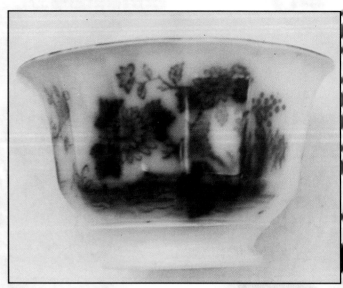

PLATE 322. Indian Waste Bowl, $200.00 – 250.00.

PLATE 323. Indian pattern on inside of Waste Bowl.

PLATE 324. Indian Sugar Bowl, $600.00 – 800.00.

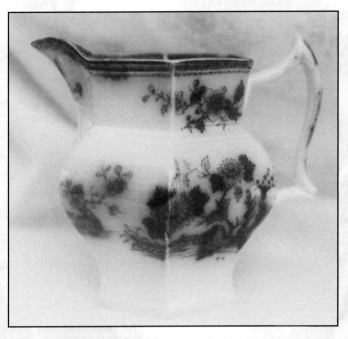

PLATE 325. Indian Creamer, $400.00 – 500.00.

PLATE 326. **Indian Jar**, J. & T. Furnival, Mark 53A, circa 1843. Plate, $175.00 – 200.00.

PLATE 327. **Indian Jar**, T. Furnival & Co., Mark 54 with "Real Iron Stone" impressed, circa 1844 – 1846. Serving Dish, 13", $1,000.00 – 1,200.00.

PLATE 328. **Indian Stone**, E. Walley, Mark 119, circa 1845 – 1856. Plate, $175.00 – 200.00.

PLATE 329. Indian Stone by Walley. Sugar Bowl, $600.00 – 800.00 (with lid).

PLATE 330. **Indian Vase**, S. & E. H., unidentified manufacturer, Mark 112, circa mid-1800s. Platter, 12", $600.00 – 800.00.

PLATE 331. **Iris**, G. L. Ashworth & Bros., Mark 17a, circa after 1862. The pattern name is not printed with the mark, but the design is the same as the one made by Corn. Chamber Pot, $300.00 – 400.00.

PLATE 332. **Iris**, W. & E. Corn, Mark 35, circa 1900 – 1904. This pattern was also made without the dark Flow Blue rim. Plate, $75.00 – 90.00.

PLATE 333. **Iris**, Doulton, Mark 43, circa 1891 – 1902. Cheese Dish, $500.00 – 600.00.

PLATE 334. **Iris**, marked E.P.P. Co. for East Palestine Pottery Co., Ohio, American, circa 1884 – 1909. "Iris" is the name printed as the pattern with the mark on this piece in spite of the fact that a turkey rather than a flower is featured. Plate, $75.00 – 100.00.

PLATE 335. **Iris**, Arthur J. Wilkinson, Mark 126, circa 1907. This is the same pattern as Lusitania by Alfred Colley. Platter, 13", $225.00 – 275.00.

PLATE 336. **Italia**, unidentified manufacturer, Mark 116a, circa after 1891. Plate, $125.00 – 150.00.

PLATE 338. **Ivanhoe**, "British Ware," unidentified manufacturer, Mark 22B, circa early 1900s. Miniature Cup and Saucer, $100.00 – 125.00.

PLATE 337. **Ivanhoe**, Josiah Wedgwood, Mark 124 with year code "AKB" impressed, circa 1899, and printed mark "Wedgwood, Etruria, England." Plate, "Rebecca Repelling the Templar," $125.00 – 150.00.

PLATE 339. **Ivory**, unmarked except for pattern name, circa early 1900s. Platter, 12", $150.00 – 200.00.

PLATE 340. **Ivy**, unmarked, see Williams I, p. 185, circa late 1800s. Pitcher, 8", $500.00 – 600.00.

PLATE 341. Ivy Pitcher, 8", in a different shape, $500.00 – 600.00.

PLATE 342. **Janette**, W. H. Grindley & Co., Mark 59, circa 1891 – 1914. Butter Pat, $40.00 – 50.00; Plate (not shown), $75.00 – 90.00.

PLATE 343. Janette by Grindley. Wash Bowl and Pitcher Set, $2,000.00 – 2,500.00.

PLATE 344. **Japan**, Edge, Malkin & Co., circa late 1800s. Set of Graduated Pitchers: left, $500.00 – 600.00; middle, $400.00 – 500.00; right, $300.00 – 400.00.

PLATE 345. **Japan**, T. Fell & Co., similar to Mark 50, circa mid-1800s. Tea Pot, $1,200.00 – 1,400.00.

PLATE 346. **Japan**, T. Rathbone & Co., Mark 105, circa 1912 – 1923. Plate, $125.00 – 150.00.

PLATE 347. **Japan Pattern**, J. & G. Meakin, Mark 88, circa after 1890. Plate, $125.00 – 150.00.

PLATE 348. **Japanese**, Minton & Hollins, Mark 94B, circa 1845 – 1868, polychrome pattern. Soup Plate, $150.00 – 175.00.

PLATE 350. **Jeddo**, W. Adams & Sons, Mark 1, circa mid-1800s. Handleless Cup and Saucer, $225.00 – 250.00.

PLATE 349. **Jardiniere**, Villeroy & Boch, German, Mark 151, circa mid-to-late 1800s. Cup and Saucer, $120.00 – 145.00.

PLATE 351. **Jedo**, Doulton, Mark 43a, circa 1891 – 1902. Plate, $100.00 – 125.00.

PLATE 352. **Jenny Lind**, Arthur J. Wilkinson, Royal Staffordshire Pottery, Mark 125, circa early 1900s. Serving Bowl, $275.00 – 300.00.

PLATE 354. **Jewel**, Johnson Bros., Mark 71, circa early 1900s. Pitchers: left, $300.00 – 400.00; right, $250.00 – 350.00.

PLATE 353. Exterior of another Serving Bowl decorated with the Jenny Lind pattern, $275.00 – 300.00.

PLATE 355. **Josephine**, Ridgways, Mark 110, circa 1912 – 1920. Platter, 10", $150.00 – 200.00.

PLATE 356. **Kaolin**, Podmore, Walker & Co., Mark 102, circa 1834 – 1859. Sugar Bowl, $800.00 – 1,000.00.

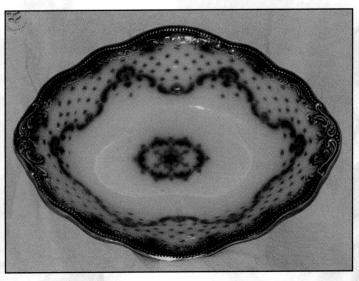

PLATE 357. **Keele**, W. H. Grindley & Co., Mark 59, circa 1891 – 1914. Serving Bowl, $125.00 – 150.00.

PLATE 358. Keele Soup Bowl, $70.00 – 85.00.

PLATE 360. **Kelvin**, Alfred Meakin, Mark 86, circa early 1900s. Butter Dish, $300.00 – 400.00 (with lid).

PLATE 359. **Kelmscott**, F. Winkle & Co., circa 1890 – 1910, polychrome pattern. Pitcher, 8", $400.00 – 500.00.

PLATE 362. **Kenworth**, Johnson Bros., similar to Mark 73, circa 1913 and after. Platter, 12", $200.00 – 250.00.

PLATE 361. **Kendal**, Ridgways, Mark 110, circa 1912 – 1920. Plate, $75.00 – 90.00.

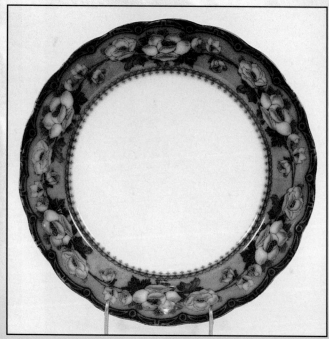

PLATE 363. **Kew**, Bourne & Leigh, Albion Pottery, Mark 22, circa early 1900s. Platter, 14", $225.00 – 275.00.

PLATE 364. **Khan**, Bishop & Stonier, Mark 20, circa 1891 – 1936. Plate, $60.00 – 75.00.

PLATE 365. **Killarney**, New Wharf Pottery, Mark 98, circa 1890 – 1894. Serving Bowl, $125.00 – 150.00.

PLATE 366. **Kin Shan**, E. Challinor & Co., Mark 30b, circa 1853 – 1860. Plate, $200.00 – 225.00, mint condition.

PLATE 368. **Kiswick**, New Wharf Pottery, Mark 98, circa 1890 – 1894. Platter, 14", $200.00 – 250.00, mint condition.

PLATE 367. **Kingston**, Keeling & Co., Ltd., Mark 78a, circa 1912 – 1936. Soup Plate, $50.00 – 60.00.

PLATE 369. **Knox**, New Wharf Pottery, Mark 98, circa 1890 – 1894. Berry Bowl, $30.00 – 40.00; Plate (not shown), $75.00 – 90.00.

PLATE 370. **Kremlin**, Samuel Alcock, Mark 14, circa 1830 – 1859. Cake Plate, $400.00 – 500.00.

PLATE 371. **Kyber**, W. Adams & Co., Mark 2, circa mid-1800s. Plate, $175.00 – 200.00.

PLATE 372. Kyber by W. Adams & Co., Mark 4, circa late 1800s to early 1900s. Gravy Boat, $225.00 – 250.00.

PLATE 373. **La Belle**, Wheeling Pottery Co., American, see Marks 168 and 169, circa after 1893 to early 1900s. Serving Plate, 11", $150.00 – 175.00.

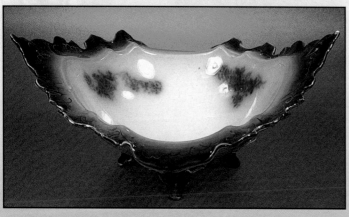

PLATE 374. La Belle footed Bowl, $400.00 – 500.00.

PLATE 375. La Belle Pitcher, 7", $500.00 – 600.00.

PLATE 376. La Belle Biscuit Jar, $400.00 – 500.00.

PLATE 377. La Belle Serving Bowl, $300.00 – 400.00.

PLATE 378. La Belle Serving Bowl with one handle, $400.00 – 500.00.

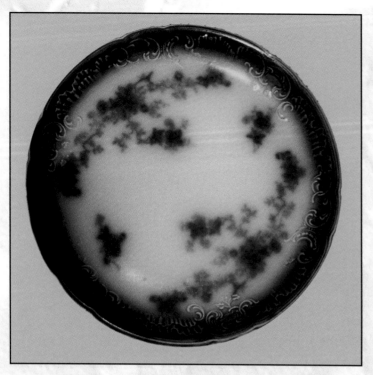

PLATE 379. La Belle Charger, 12", $200.00 – 250.00.

PLATE 380. La Belle Chocolate Pot, $800.00 – 1,000.00.

PLATE 381. La Belle Butter Dish, $500.00 – 600.00.

PLATE 382. La Belle Serving Bowl with curved handle, $400.00 – 500.00.

PLATE 383. La Belle Sugar Bowl, $200.00 – 250.00.

PLATE 384. La Belle Syrup or Molasses Pitcher, $600.00 – 700.00, with lid, mint condition.

PLATE 385. La Belle Tray, 11", $500.00 – 600.00.

PLATE 386. **Ladas**, unidentified manufacturer, circa early 1900s. The pattern name is legible on this example, but the factory mark is not. This is not the same Ladas pattern made by Ridgways (see Williams I, p. 109). Chamber Pot with Lid, $500.00 – 600.00.

PLATE 387. **Lahore**, unidentified manufacturer, Mark 135, circa early 1900s. Mark 117, with a "W" under the pattern name, is also found with this pattern. Plate, $150.00 – 175.00.

PLATE 388. **Lakewood**, New Wharf Pottery, similar to Mark 98, circa 1890 – 1894. This is the same pattern as Persian by Johnson Bros. Plate, $75.00 – 90.00.

PLATE 390. **Lakewood**, Wood & Son, Mark 131, circa 1891 – 1907. Wood & Son, successor to New Wharf Pottery, continued the Lakewood pattern. Tureen, $600.00 – 700.00; Ladle, $175.00 – 225.00.

PLATE 389. Lakewood by New Wharf Pottery, Mark 98. Cup and Saucer, $100.00 – 125.00.

PLATE 391. Lakewood by Wood & Son. Sugar Bowl, $175.00 – 225.00.

PLATE 392. **Lancaster**, Bishop & Stonier, Mark 20, circa early 1900s. Plate, $65.00 – 80.00.

PLATE 394. **Larch**, Sampson Hancock & Sons, Mark 63, circa 1906 – 1912. Platter, 12", $150.00 – 200.00.

PLATE 393. **Lancaster**, New Wharf Pottery, Mark 98, circa 1890 – 1894. Cup and Saucer, $100.00 – 125.00.

PLATE 396. Le Pavot by Grindley. Covered Vegetable Dish, $275.00 – 325.00.

PLATE 395. **Le Pavot**, W. H. Grindley & Co., Mark 60, circa 1891 – 1914. Plate, $65.00 – 80.00.

PLATE 398. **Leicester**, Sampson Hancock & Sons, Mark 65, circa 1906 – 1912. Platter, 15", $350.00 – 400.00.

PLATE 397. **"Leaf & Worm,"** unmarked, hand-painted pattern, circa late 1800s. Plate, $125.00 – 150.00.

PLATE 399. **Leipsic**, J. Clementson, Mark 31A, circa 1840 – 1864. Rectangular Serving Dish, $400.00 – 500.00.

PLATE 400. **Lily**, Adderley, circa late 1800s, see Williams II, p. 141. Pair of Vases, 9", $1,000.00 – 1,200.00 pair.

PLATE 401. **Limoges**, Wood & Son, Mark 131, circa 1891 – 1907. Plate, $75.00 – 90.00.

PLATE 402. Limoges Soup Bowl, $75.00 – 90.00.

PLATE 403. Limoges Dessert Bowl, $35.00 – 45.00; Bread and Butter Plates, $25.00 – 35.00 each.

PLATE 404. Limoges Cup and Saucer, $100.00 – 125.00.

PLATE 405. Limoges Creamer, $175.00 – 225.00; Sugar Bowl, $200.00 – 250.00; Spoon Holder, $100.00 – 125.00.

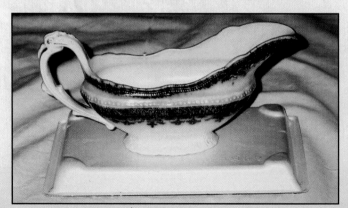

PLATE 406. Limoges Gravy Boat, $125.00 – 145.00.

PLATE 407. Limoges Covered Butter Dish, $400.00 – 500.00.

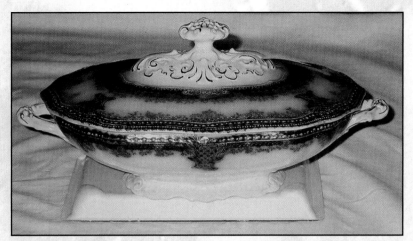

PLATE 408. Limoges Covered Serving Bowl, $300.00 – 350.00.

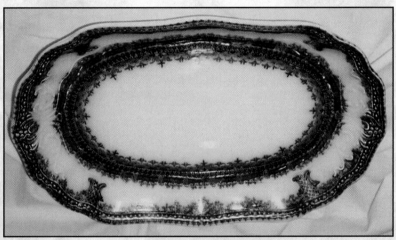

PLATE 409. Limoges Platter, 14", $250.00 – 300.00.

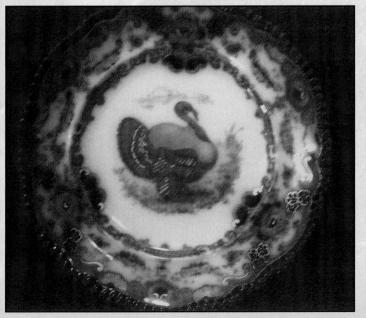

PLATE 410. **Lincoln**, Bishop & Stonier, Mark 20, circa early 1900s, polychrome pattern. This is another example (see Iris by East Palestine Pottery Co.) of the center pattern, a turkey, having no relationship with the name of the pattern. The pattern name, however, could refer to the border pattern (like Watteau by Doulton). Plate, $125.00 – 150.00.

PLATE 411. **Linnea**, Grimwades, Mark 57, circa after 1903. Soup Plate, $50.00 – 65.00.

PLATE 412. **Lobelia**, George Phillips, Mark 101, with a Registry Mark for 1845. Pitcher, 6", $300.00 – 400.00.

PLATE 413. **Lois**, New Wharf Pottery, Mark 99, circa 1890 – 1894. Plate, $75.00 – 90.00.

PLATE 414. **Lonsdale**, Samuel Ford & Co., Mark 50A, circa early 1900s. Covered Serving Dish, $300.00 – 350.00.

PLATE 415. Lonsdale by Samuel Ford & Co. Tray, 11", $200.00 – 250.00.

PLATE 416. **Lonsdale**, Ridgways, Mark 110, circa 1912 – 1920. Covered Serving Dish, $300.00 – 350.00.

PLATE 417. Lonsdale by Ridgways. Serving Bowl, $150.00 – 175.00.

PLATE 418. **Lorne**, W. H. Grindley & Co., Mark 59, circa 1891 – 1914. Serving Bowl, $125.00 – 150.00.

PLATE 419. **Lotus**, unidentified manufacturer, Mark 136, circa early 1900s. Serving Bowl, $125.00 – 150.00.

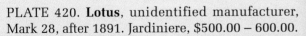

PLATE 420. **Lotus**, unidentified manufacturer, Mark 28, after 1891. Jardiniere, $500.00 – 600.00.

PLATE 421. **Louise**, New Wharf Pottery, Mark 98, circa 1890 – 1894. Serving Bowl, $150.00 – 175.00.

PLATE 422. **Lucania**, Edward Clarke, Mark 31, circa 1877 – 1887. Plate, $75.00 – 90.00.

PLATE 423. **Lugano**, Ridgways, Mark 110, circa 1912 – 1920. Plate, $75.00 – 90.00.

PLATE 424. Lugano by Ridgways. Covered Serving Bowl, $300.00 – 350.00.

PLATE 425. **Lusitania**, Alfred Colley, Ltd., Mark 33a, circa 1909 – 1914. This is the same pattern as Iris by A. J. Wilkinson, Royal Staffordshire Pottery. Plate, $65.00 – 80.00.

PLATE 426. **Luzerne**, Mercer Pottery, American, Mark 166a, circa early 1900s. This is the same pattern as Waldorf by New Wharf Pottery. Soup Plate, $100.00 – 125.00.

PLATE 428. **Mabel**, Charles Allerton & Sons, Mark 16, circa 1903 – 1912. Cup and Saucer, $120.00 – 140.00.

PLATE 427. **Lyndhurst**, W. H. Grindley & Co., Mark 59, circa 1891 – 1914. Egg Cup, $100.00 – 125.00.

PLATE 429. **Madras**, Davenport, Mark 37b, circa 1840s. Cake Plate, $300.00 – 400.00.

PLATE 430. **Madras**, Doulton, Mark 42, circa 1891 – 1902. Plate, $150.00 – 175.00.

PLATE 431. Madras by Doulton, Mark 43. Platter, 16", $400.00 – 500.00.

PLATE 432. Madras by Doulton, Mark 47. Hot Water Plate, $600.00 – 700.00.

PLATE 433. Madras by Doulton. Tureen, $800.00 – 1,000.00; Tray, $400.00 – 500.00; Ladle, $200.00 – 250.00.

PLATE 434. **Madras**, Minton & Co., year code for 1843. Pitcher, 18", $1,500.00 – 2,000.00.

PLATE 435. **Madras**, marked "O.H.E.C., Stone China," Old Hall, circa 1861 – 1886. (See Godden Marks 2917 and 2919). The same pattern was made earlier by Minton, see the previous example. Plate, $125.00 – 150.00.

PLATE 436. **Madras**, Wood & Son, Mark 131, circa 1891 – 1907. The same pattern and name was used by New Wharf Pottery, predecessor to Wood & Son. An unidentified manufacturer, Mark 141, also made this pattern. Soup Plate, $70.00 – 85.00.

157

PLATE 437. **Maidstone**, T. Rathbone, Mark 105, circa 1912 – 1923. Large Pitcher, $500.00 – 600.00.

PLATE 438. **Maltese**, marked "C & B" with "L," possibly Cotton & Barlow, Longton (see Godden Mark 1116, circa 1850 – 1855, and see Williams I, p. 37). Cake Plate, $400.00 – 500.00.

PLATE 439. **Mandarin**, Pountney & Co., Ltd., Mark 104, circa early 1900s. Plate, $100.00 – 125.00.

PLATE 440. **Mandarin**, Wiltshaw & Robinson, Mark 127, circa early 1900s. There is no pattern name with this mark, but the examples in Plates 440 – 442 are the same as the Mandarin pattern by Pountney, although the full pattern may not be on all pieces. Cheese Dish, $300.00 – 400.00.

PLATE 441. Mandarin by Wiltshaw & Robinson. Tea Pot, $300.00 – 400.00; Trivet, with full pattern, $150.00 – 175.00.

PLATE 442. Mandarin by Wiltshaw & Robinson. Pitcher with Metal Lid, $400.00 – 500.00.

PLATE 443. **Manhattan**, Henry Alcock, Mark 11, circa 1891 – 1900. Soup Plate, $70.00 – 85.00.

PLATE 444. **Manilla**, Podmore, Walker & Co., Mark 102, circa 1834 – 1859. Plate, $200.00 – 225.00.

PLATE 445. Manilla handleless Cup and Saucer, $225.00 – 275.00.

PLATE 446. Manilla Serving Dish, $1,000.00 – 1,200.00.

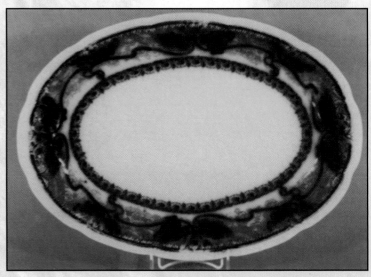

PLATE 448. **Manskillan**, Wood & Son, Mark 131, circa 1891 – 1907. Platter, 16", $300.00 – 400.00.

PLATE 447. Manilla Bowl and Pitcher Set, $5,000.00 – 6,000.00.

PLATE 449. **Marechal Neil**, W. H. Grindley & Co., Mark 59, circa 1891 – 1914. Soup Plate, $70.00 – 85.00.

PLATE 451. Marguerite by Grindley. Compote, $400.00 – 450.00.

PLATE 450. **Marguerite**, W. H. Grindley & Co., Mark 60, circa 1891 – 1914. Plate, $70.00 – 85.00.

PLATE 452. **Marie**, W. H. Grindley & Co., Mark 59, circa 1891 – 1914. Plate, $75.00 – 90.00.

PLATE 453. Marie by Grindley. Sugar Bowl, $200.00 – 250.00.

PLATE 454. **The Marquis**, W. H. Grindley & Co., Mark 59 or 60a can be found with this pattern, circa 1891 – 1914. Plate, $75.00 – 90.00.

PLATE 455. **Martha**, Upper Hanley Pottery, Mark 115, circa 1895 – 1900. Soup Plate, $45.00 – 60.00.

PLATE 456. Martha by Upper Hanley Pottery. Bone Dish, $75.00 – 100.00.

PLATE 457. **Mazara**, W. Adams & Co., Mark 7, circa early 1900s. Plate, $100.00 – 125.00.

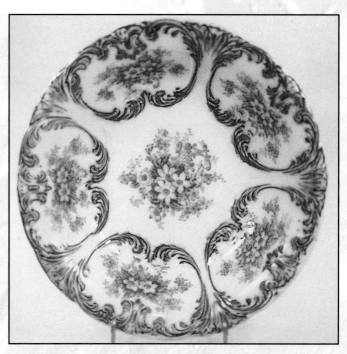

PLATE 458. **Meissen**, T. Furnival & Sons, impressed name and anchor mark and "J.R. Gibney, New York," a printed importer mark, circa 1878. Soup Bowl, $100.00 – 125.00.

PLATE 459. **Meissen**, F. A. Mehlem, German, Marks 149 and 150, circa early 1900s. Serving Bowl, $140.00 – 165.00.

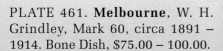

PLATE 460. **Meissen**, unidentified manufacturer, Mark 137, after 1891. This is the same pattern as Holland by Johnson Bros. and Onion by various manufacturers. Platter, 13", $325.00 – 375.00.

PLATE 461. **Melbourne**, W. H. Grindley, Mark 60, circa 1891 – 1914. Bone Dish, $75.00 – 100.00.

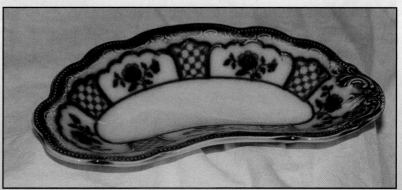

PLATE 462. **Melrose**, Doulton, Mark 42, circa 1891 – 1902. Plate, $65.00 – 80.00.

PLATE 463. **Melrose**, New Wharf Pottery, Mark 98, circa 1890 – 1894. Soup Bowl, $70.00 – 85.00.

PLATE 464. **Melsary**, Booths, Mark 20B, circa 1906. Platter, 22", with deep well, $500.00 – 600.00.

PLATE 465. **Melton**, Ford & Sons, circa 1890s to early 1900s. Pitcher, 8", $500.00 – 600.00.

PLATE 466. **Melville**, Registry Mark circa 1891, illegible factory mark with pattern name. Platter, 18", $300.00 – 350.00.

PLATE 467. **Messina**, Brown-Westhead, Moore & Co., Mark 23a, circa 1895 – 1904. Soup Plate, $75.00 – 90.00.

PLATE 468. **Messina**, Alfred Meakin, Ltd., Mark 86, circa early 1900s. Tureen, $300.00 – 400.00.

PLATE 469. **Mikado**, Arthur J. Wilkinson, crown mark with "A. J. Wilkinson Ltd., England," circa 1891 to early 1900s. Plate, $65.00 – 80.00.

PLATE 470. **Milan**, Ford & Sons, Mark 51, circa 1893 – 1907. Gravy Boat and Tray, $225.00 – 275.00 set.

PLATE 471. **Milan**, W. H. Grindley & Co., Mark 59, circa 1891 – 1914. Soup Tureen, $300.00 – 400.00; Ladle, $150.00 – 175.00.

PLATE 472. **Mona**, Minton & Boyle, Mark 94a, circa 1836 – 1841. Tureen, $1,000.00 – 1,200.00; Tray, $500.00 – 600.00.

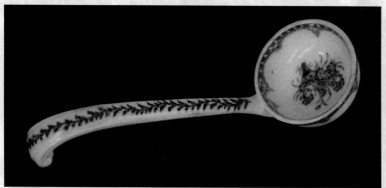

PLATE 473. Mona by Minton & Boyle. Ladle, $250.00 – 300.00.

PLATE 474. **Monarch**, Myott, Son & Co., Mark 97, circa 1907 and after. Pitcher, 5", $200.00 – 250.00.

PLATE 475. **Monarch**, New Wharf Pottery, Mark 98, circa 1890 – 1894. Plate, $75.00 – 90.00.

PLATE 476. **Mongolia**, unmarked, circa mid-to-late 1800s, attributed to Mark 49B, F. & W., unidentified manufacturer (Plate 200 in my *Second Series* shows this pattern on an example with Mark 49B). Tureen, $800.00 – 1,000.00; Tray, $400.00 – 500.00; Ladle, $175.00 – 200.00.

PLATE 477. **Mongolia**, Johnson Bros., Mark 73, circa 1913 and after. Platter, 11", $250.00 – 300.00.

PLATE 478. Mongolia by Johnson Bros. Covered Serving Bowl, $350.00 – 400.00.

PLATE 479. **Montana**, Johnson Bros., Mark 71, circa early 1900s. Plate, $65.00 – 80.00.

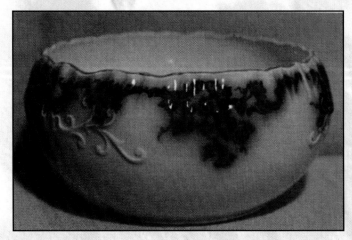

PLATE 480. **Morning Glory**, Thomas Hughes & Son, Mark 68a, circa 1895 – 1910. Rose Bowl, $200.00 – 250.00.

PLATE 481. **Morning Glory**, unmarked, see Williams II, p. 147. Handleless Cup and Saucer, $150.00 – 175.00.

PLATE 482. **Muriel**, unmarked, attributed to Upper Hanley Pottery, circa 1895 – 1910, see Williams I, p. 155. Serving Bowl, $150.00 – 175.00.

PLATE 483. **Naida**, Upper Hanley Pottery, Mark 115, circa 1895 – 1900. Plate (with an advertisement for "Crawford Cooking Ranges"), $60.00 – 75.00.

PLATE 484. **Nankin**, unmarked, attributed to Brown-Westhead, Moore & Co., circa late 1800s (see Godden Mark 681 and Wiliams II, p. 53). Tea Pot, $800.00 – 1,000.00.

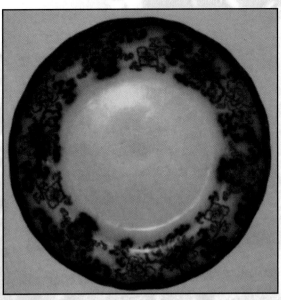

PLATE 485. **Nankin**, Doulton, Mark 42, circa 1891 – 1902. Plate, $70.00 – 85.00.

PLATE 486. **Nankin Jar**, Ashworth, Mark 17 (without the crown), and with printed pattern name, circa 1862 – 1880. Large Serving Dish, $1,000.00 – 1,200.00.

PLATE 487. Nankin Jar, unmarked, attributed to Ashworth. Pitcher, $225.00 – 275.00.

PLATE 488. Nankin Jar by Ashworth. Plate, $100.00 – 125.00.

PLATE 489. **Nankin Jar**, Doulton, circa early 1900s, polychrome pattern. Compote, $800.00 – 1,000.00.

PLATE 490. **Navarre**, Wedgwood & Co., Mark 121a, circa 1900 – 1908. Plate, $75.00 – 90.00.

PLATE 491. **Neopolitan**, Johnson Bros., Mark 70, circa early 1900s. Plate, $50.00 – 65.00.

PLATE 492. **Nile**, Till & Sons, Mark 113A, circa 1880 – 1891. Covered Serving Bowl, $300.00 – 350.00.

PLATE 493. **Ning Po**, R. Hall & Co., see Williams I, p. 39 and Godden Mark 1890a, circa 1845. Plate, $200.00 – 225.00.

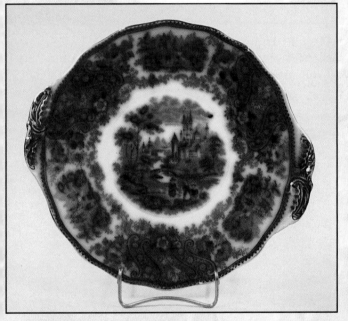

PLATE 494. **Non Pareil**, Burgess & Leigh, Mark 25, circa 1891 – 1919. Cake Plate, $400.00 – 500.00.

PLATE 495. **Norah**, T. Rathbone & Co., Mark 105, circa 1912 – 1923. Plate, $75.00 – 90.00.

PLATE 496. **Norbury**, Doulton, Mark 44, circa early 1900s. Wash bowl and Pitcher Set, $2,500.00 – 3,000.00; Toothbrush Holder, $200.00 – 225.00; Covered Soap Dish, $225.00 – 250.00; Chamber Pot, $350.00 – 450.00.

PLATE 497. **Normandy**, Johnson Bros., Mark 70, circa early 1900s. Cup and Saucer, $100.00 – 125.00.

PLATE 498. **Old Castles**, Henry Alcock & Co., Mark 11a in green with pattern name printed in a separate blue mark with a Registry Date circa 1913. Plate, $125.00 – 150.00.

PLATE 499. **Olga**, Ridgways, Mark 109, circa 1905 – 1920. Plate, $65.00 – 80.00.

PLATE 500. **The Olympia**, W. H. Grindley & Co., Mark 61, circa 1914 – 1925. Cup and Saucer, $75.00 – 100.00.

PLATE 502. **Oregon**, T. J. & J. Mayer, Mark 84, circa 1843 to mid-1850s. Soup Plate, $200.00 – 225.00.

PLATE 501. **Oregon**, Johnson Bros., Mark 71, circa early 1900s. Plate, $70.00 – 85.00.

PLATE 503. Oregon by Mayer. Tea Pot, $1,200.00 – 1,400.00.

PLATE 504. **Oriental**, Samuel Alcock, Mark 14a, circa 1830 – 1859. Plate, $175.00 – 225.00.

PLATE 505. Oriental by Alcock. Sauce Tureen, $500.00 – 600.00.

PLATE 506. **Oriental**, New Wharf Pottery, Mark 100a, circa 1890 – 1894. Plate, $125.00 – 150.00.

PLATE 508. Oriental by Ridgways. Creamer, $200.00 – 250.00.

PLATE 507. **Oriental**, Ridgways, Mark 108, circa 1891 to early 1900s. Platter, 19", $1,000.00 – 1,200.00.

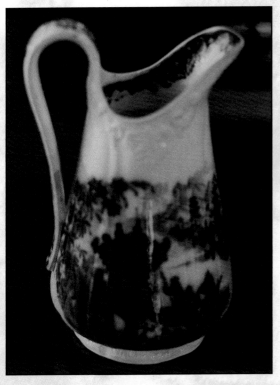

PLATE 510. **Orleans**, Thomas Dimmock, Mark 39a, circa 1828 – 1859. Platter, 16", $300.00 – 350.00, mint condition.

PLATE 509. **Oriental**, Rorstrand, Swedish, see Williams III, p. 10, circa 1880s. Pitcher, 6", $400.00 – 500.00.

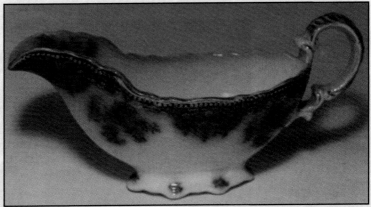

PLATE 512. **Osborne**, W. H. Grindley & Co., Mark 60, circa 1891 – 1914. Gravy Boat, $120.00 – 145.00.

PLATE 511. **Ormonde**, Alfred Meakin, Mark 86, circa early 1900s. Pitcher, 7", $400.00 – 500.00.

PLATE 514. Osborne by Ridgways. Tea Cup and Saucer and Demitasse Cup and Saucer, $100.00 – 125.00 each.

PLATE 513. **Osborne**, Ridgways, Mark 109, circa 1905 – 1920. Plate, $65.00 – 80.00.

PLATE 515. **Oxford**, Ford & Sons, Mark 51, circa 1893 – 1907. Soup Plate, $70.00 – 85.00.

PLATE 516. **Oxford**, Johnson Bros., Mark 70, circa early 1900s. Plate, $70.00 – 85.00.

PLATE 517. Oxford by Johnson Bros. Berry Bowl without center pattern, $60.00 – 75.00.

PLATE 518. **Oyama**, Doulton, Mark 44a, circa 1906. Pitcher, 6", $400.00 – 500.00.

PLATE 519. **Pagoda**, J. & G. Meakin, Mark 90, circa 1912 and after. Covered Serving Dish, $275.00 – 325.00.

PLATE 520. **Paisley**, Mercer Pottery Company, Trenton, New Jersey, American, Mark 166, circa late 1800s. Plate, $75.00 – 90.00.

PLATE 521. **Pansy**, unmarked, attributed to Johnson Bros., circa early 1900s, see Williams II, p. 150. Pitcher, 9", $500.00 – 600.00.

PLATE 522. **Paqueminot**, Ridgways, Mark 110, circa 1912 – 1920. Plate, $75.00 – 90.00.

PLATE 523. **Parapette**, Keller & Guerin, French, Mark 145, circa late 1800s. Cup and Saucer, $100.00 – 125.00.

PLATE 524. **Paris**, New Wharf Pottery, Mark 98, circa 1890 – 1894. Plate, $75.00 – 90.00.

PLATE 525. **Peach**, Johnson Bros., Mark 70, circa early 1900s. Berry Bowl, $25.00 – 35.00; Plate (not shown), $65.00 – 80.00.

PLATE 526. **Pekin**, Davenport, Mark 37a, circa mid-1800s. Plate, $125.00 – 150.00.

PLATE 527. **Pekin**, Thomas Dimmock, Mark 39a, circa 1828 – 1859. Plate, $125.00 – 150.00; Handleless Cup and Saucer, $200.00 – 250.00; Cup Plate, $100.00 – 125.00.

PLATE 528. **Pekin** (without center pattern), Johnson Bros., with printed patent date, "Pat. Oct. 21/02." Plate, $60.00 – 75.00; Cup and Saucer, $100.00 – 125.00.

PLATE 529. Pekin by Johnson Bros. Pitcher, 6",
$300.00 – 400.00.

PLATE 530. **Pekin**, marked "Albert E. Jones," see
Williams I, p. 43, circa 1905 – 1929. Plate, $100.00 –
125.00.

PLATE 531. **Pekin**, Arthur J. Wilkinson, Royal
Staffordshire Pottery mark (not shown), circa early
1900s. This example only has the border pattern of
Pekin, see Williams I, p. 44 for the center pattern.
Plate, $65.00 – 80.00.

PLATE 532. **Pelew**, E. Challinor, Mark 30, circa 1842 –
1867. Plate, $200.00 – 225.00.

PLATE 533. **Pembroke**, Bishop & Stonier, Mark 20, circa early 1900s. Soup Plate, $60.00 – 75.00.

PLATE 534. **Penang** (1), William Ridgway, Mark 107, circa 1830 – 1834. Plate, $225.00 – 250.00.

PLATE 535. **Penang** (2), William Ridgway, Oriental style mark with pattern name (not shown), circa early 1830s. This Penang pattern by Ridgway is different from Plate 534. This pattern is also the same as Formosa by William Ridgway, see Williams I, p. 45. Platter, 16", $1,200.00 – 1,400.00.

PLATE 536. **Percy**, attributed to Francis Morley, circa mid-1800s, see Williams III, p. 18. Jam Pot with Hinged Metal Lid, $175.00 – 225.00.

PLATE 537. Interior of Jam Pot in Plate 536.

PLATE 538. **Pergolesi**, Brown-Westhead, Moore & Co., Mark 23 and a Registry Mark circa 1886. Platter, 19", $500.00 – 600.00.

PLATE 539. **Persian**, Johnson Bros., Mark 70, circa early 1900s. This is the same pattern as Lakewood by New Wharf Pottery. Plate, $75.00 – 90.00.

PLATE 540. **Persian Moss**, Mark 148, German, circa early 1900s, see Williams I, p. 195. Plate, $70.00 – 85.00.

PLATE 541. **Persian Spray**, Doulton, Mark 43, circa 1891 – 1902. Ewer, $500.00 – 600.00.

PLATE 542. **Peruvian**, John Wedge Wood, Mark 130, circa 1841 – 1860. Plate, $175.00 – 200.00.

PLATE 543. **Petunia**, manufacturer not identified; the mark is like Mark 62, except it has the initials "C. & H." rather than "H - Bros." Jardiniere, 6½" h x 8½" d, pattern enhanced with gold, $500.00 – 600.00.

PLATE 544. **Petunia**, H. Bros., unidentified manufacturer, Mark 62, circa early 1900s. The pattern is the same one as Petunia by "C. & H.," also an unidentified company, see Mark 28. Hot Water Jug with Liner, $500.00 – 600.00.

PLATE 545. **Petunia**, Wiltshaw & Robinson, Mark 127, circa early 1900s. Square Covered Dish, $325.00 – 375.00.

PLATE 546. **Pilgrims Landing**, The French China Co., American, Mark 162, circa early 1900s. Oval Bowl, $175.00 – 225.00.

PLATE 547. Pilgrims Landing by The French China Co. Plate, $75.00 – 100.00.

PLATE 548. **Plymouth**, New Wharf Pottery, Mark 98, 1890 – 1894. Bacon Platter, 8", $125.00 – 150.00.

PLATE 549. Plymouth by New Wharf Pottery. Pitcher, 6", $300.00 – 400.00.

PLATE 550. **Poppea**, Grimwades, Mark 56, circa 1886 – 1900. Jardiniere and Pedestal, $3,000.00 – 4,000.00.

PLATE 551. **Poppy**, W. Adams & Co., after 1881 (see Williams II, p. 196). Serving Bowl, $120.00 – 145.00.

PLATE 552. **Poppy**, Doulton, Mark 44, circa early 1900s. Pitchers: left, 6", $225.00 – 275.00; center, 8", $325.00 – 375.00; right, 7", $250.00 – 300.00.

PLATE 553. **Poppy**, W. H. Grindley & Co., Mark 60, circa 1891 – 1914. Tureen, $300.00 – 400.00; Platter, $150.00 – 175.00.

PLATE 555. "**Poppy**," unmarked, see Snyder 2000, p. 180, circa late 1800s. Dresser Set, $1,400.00 – 1,600.00 set.

PLATE 554. **Poppy**, New Wharf Pottery, Mark 99, circa 1890 – 1894. Plate, $75.00 – 90.00.

PLATE 556. "**Poppy**" Wash Set. Bowl and Pitcher, $2,000.00 – 2,500.00. Chamber Pot, $300.00 – 400.00.

PLATE 557. **Portman**, W. H. Grindley & Co., Mark 60, circa 1891 – 1914. Plate, $70.00 – 85.00.

PLATE 558. **Portsmouth**, New Wharf Pottery, Mark 98, circa 1890 – 1894. Plate, $75.00 – 90.00.

PLATE 559. **Princess**, T. Rathbone, Mark 105, circa 1912 – 1923. Sauce Tureen, $300.00 – 400.00.

PLATE 560. **Princeton**, Johnson Bros., Mark 70, circa early 1900s. Butter Pat, $35.00 – 40.00.

PLATE 561. Princeton by Johnson Bros. Plate, $70.00 – 85.00.

PLATE 562. **Progress**, W. H. Grindley & Co., Mark 59, circa 1891 – 1914. Berry Dish, $25.00 – 35.00. Plate (not shown), $60.00 – 75.00.

187

PLATE 564. **Quinton**, unidentified manufacturer, illegible impressed mark plus pattern name, circa early 1900s. Tea Pot, $300.00 – 350.00.

PLATE 563. **Quebec**, unidentified manufacturer, German, Mark 147, circa after 1891. Plate, $65.00 – 80.00.

PLATE 565. **Raleigh**, Burgess & Leigh, Mark 27, circa early 1900s. Covered Serving Dish, $400.00 – 500.00.

PLATE 566. **Rebecca**, George Jones & Sons, circa early 1900s (see Williams I, p. 197). Plate, $70.00 – 85.00.

PLATE 567. **The Regal**, W. H. Grindley & Co., Mark 61, circa 1914 – 1925. Bone Dish, $75.00 – 100.00.

PLATE 568. **Regala**, Thomas Hughes & Son, Mark 68a, circa 1895 – 1910. Plate $65.00 – 80.00.

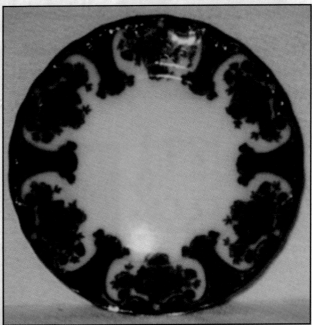

PLATE 569. **Regent**, Alfred Meakin, Mark 87, circa early 1900s. Covered Serving Bowl, $275.00 – 325.00.

PLATE 570. **Regent**, unidentified manufacturer, pattern name is printed within a wreath with "England," circa after 1891. Plate, $70.00 – 85.00.

PLATE 571. **Regina**, J. & G. Meakin, Mark 90, circa 1912 and after. Soup Bowl, $70.00 – 85.00.

PLATE 572. **Return of the Mayflower**, Wedgwood & Co., impressed mark (not shown), after 1860. Commemorative Plate, $125.00 – 150.00.

PLATE 573. **Rhine**, Thomas Dimmock, Mark 39, circa 1828 – 1859. Platter, 14", $800.00 – 1,000.00.

PLATE 574. **Rhine**, unidentified manufacturer, illegible factory mark with pattern name, circa early 1900s. Serving Bowl, $100.00 – 125.00.

PLATE 575. **Rhoda Gardens**, Hackwood, Mark 62A, circa early-to-mid-1800s. Plate, $200.00 – 225.00.

PLATE 576. **Rhone**, Thomas Furnival & Co., similar to Mark 54, circa 1844 – 1846. Tea Pot, $1,000.00 – 1,200.00 (with lid).

PLATE 577. Rhone, illegible impressed mark. The pattern is the same as in the previous picture. Pitcher, 6", $800.00 – 1,000.00.

PLATE 578. **Richmond**, unmarked, attributed to Ford & Sons, circa 1893 – 1907 (see Williams III, p. 58). Platter, 12", $325.00 – 375.00.

PLATE 579. **Richmond**, Johnson Bros., Mark 72, circa early 1900s. Berry Bowl, $25.00 – 35.00. Plate (not shown), $65.00 – 80.00.

PLATE 580. **Rio**, Ford & Sons, Mark 52a, circa after 1908. Rectangular Tray, 12", $150.00 – 200.00.

PLATE 581. **Rock**, E. Challinor, Mark 30a, circa 1842 – 1867. Plate, $200.00 – 225.00.

PLATE 582. **Roma**, Wedgwood & Co., Mark 121a, circa 1900 – 1908. Covered Serving Dish, $350.00 – 400.00.

PLATE 583. **Romance**, unmarked, see Williams II, p. 103, circa late 1800s. Jam or Honey Dish, $100.00 – 125.00. Plate (not shown), $125.00 – 150.00.

PLATE 584. **Rose**, W. H. Grindley, Mark 60, circa 1891 – 1914. Plate, $60.00 – 75.00.

PLATE 585. **Rose**, Myott, Son & Co., Mark 96, circa early 1900s. Jardiniere, $600.00 – 700.00.

PLATE 586. **Rose**, Ridgways, Mark 110, circa 1912 – 1920. Plate, $70.00 – 85.00.

PLATE 587. **Roses and Ribbons**, John Maddock & Sons, Mark 83, circa 1880 – 1896. Berry Dish and Drainer, $300.00 – 400.00.

PLATE 588. **Roseville**, John Maddock & Sons, Mark 83, circa 1880 – 1896. This is the same pattern as Floral by T. Hughes, Senator by J. Dimmock, and Royal Blue and Balmoral by Burgess & Campbell (an American factory). Plate, $75.00 – 90.00.

PLATE 589. **Roslyn**, Alfred Colley & Co., Ltd., Mark 33, circa 1909 – 1914. Plate, $70.00 – 85.00.

PLATE 590. **Roxbury**, Ridgways, Mark 110, circa 1912 – 1920. Pitcher, 6", $225.00 – 275.00.

PLATE 592. **Royal**, unmarked but attributed to Wood & Son, circa 1891 – 1907. Wash Bowl and Pitcher Set, $2,000.00 – 2,500.00.

PLATE 591. **Roy**, unidentified manufacturer, marked only with pattern name, circa late 1800s to early 1900s. Pitcher, 8", $500.00 – 600.00.

PLATE 594. Royal Blue Covered Serving Bowl, $300.00 – 350.00.

PLATE 593. **Royal Blue**, Burgess & Campbell, American. This pattern may be found with Marks 156, 157, or 158, circa late 1800s to early 1900s. This is the same pattern as Balmoral by Burgess & Campbell, Floral by Thomas Hughes, Roseville by John Maddock, and Senator by J. Dimmock. Plate, $100.00 – 125.00.

PLATE 595. Royal Blue Covered Serving Bowl with gold enhancement on the pattern, $300.00 – 350.00.

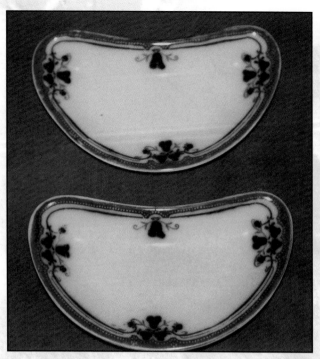

PLATE 597. **Rudyard**, F. Winkle & Co., Mark 128, circa 1890 – 1910. Butter Dish, $300.00 – 400.00.

PLATE 596. **Royston**, Johnson Bros., Mark 70, circa early 1900s. Bone Dishes: top, $75.00 – 100.00; bottom, $100.00 – 125.00.

PLATE 598. **Rugge**, J. Kent, Mark 79, circa 1910. This is the same pattern as Delft by Mintons, Delph by Wood & Son, and Madras by Upper Hanley Pottery. Serving Bowl, $150.00 – 175.00.

PLATE 599. **Ruskin**, Ford & Sons, Mark 51, circa 1893 – 1907. Plate, $100.00 – 125.00.

PLATE 600. **Ruth**, Willets, American, Mark 170, circa 1890. Plate, $100.00 – 125.00.

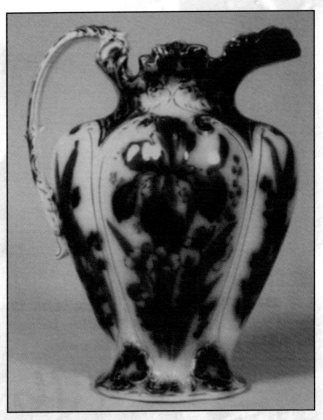

PLATE 601. **Salisbury**, Ford & Sons, Mark 51a, circa 1893 – 1907. Pitcher to Wash Set, $1,200.00 – 1,400.00.

PLATE 602. Salisbury, Bowl to Wash Set. $1,000.00 – 1,200.00.

PLATE 603. **Sandon**, Ford & Sons, Mark 51, circa 1893 – 1907. Plate, $70.00 – 85.00.

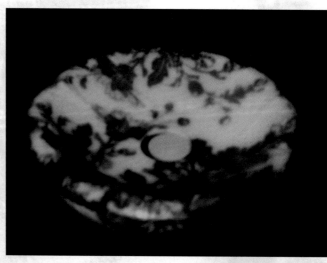

PLATE 604. **Saskia**, Ridgways, Mark 109, circa 1905 – 1920. Pieces of a Wash Set: Mug, $125.00 – 150.00; Pitcher, 8", $400.00 – 500.00; Covered Soap Dish with Liner, $250.00 – 300.00.

PLATE 605. Saskia by Ridgways. Cuspidor, $1,200.00 – 1,500.00.

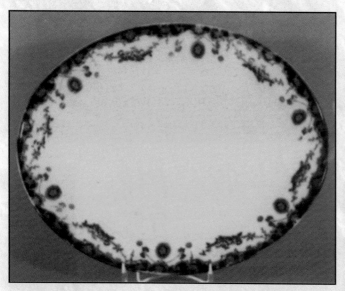

PLATE 607. **Savoy**, Johnson Bros., Mark 73, circa 1913 and after. Sugar Bowl, $175.00 – 225.00, with lid.

PLATE 606. **Savoy**, Empire Porcelain Co., Mark 49A, circa 1912 – 1928. Platter, 13", $200.00 – 250.00.

PLATE 608. **Savoy**, New Wharf Pottery, Mark 98, circa 1890 – 1894. Platter, 16", $275.00 – 325.00.

PLATE 609. **Scinde**, John & George Alcock, Mark 13, circa 1839 – 1846. Plate, $200.00 – 225.00.

PLATE 610. **Scinde**, T. Walker, marked "T. Walker" over "Ironstone" with pattern name (mark not shown), circa mid-1800s. Plate, $175.00 – 200.00.

PLATE 611. **Sefton**, Myott, Son & Co., Mark 97, circa 1907 and after. Gravy Boat, $120.00 – 145.00.

PLATE 612. **Sefton**, Ridgways, Mark 109, circa 1905 – 1920. Berry Dish, $25.00 – 35.00. Plate (not shown), $60.00 – 75.00.

PLATE 614. **Seville**, New Wharf Pottery, Mark 98, circa 1890 – 1894. The successor to New Wharf Pottery, Wood & Son, continued this pattern. Covered Vegetable Dish, $350.00 – 400.00.

PLATE 613. **Senator**, J. Dimmock, Mark 38, circa 1878 – 1904. This is the same pattern as Floral by Thomas Hughes, Roseville by John Maddock, and Balmoral and Royal Blue by Burgess & Campbell (American). Plate, $75.00 – 90.00.

PLATE 615. **Seville**, Wood & Son, Mark 131, circa after 1891 – 1907. Bone Dish, $100.00 – 125.00.

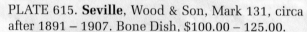

PLATE 616. Seville by Wood & Son. Butter Dish, $400.00 – 500.00.

PLATE 617. **Shangay**, unidentified manufacturer, unmarked except for pattern name, circa mid-1800s. This is the same pattern as Shanghai and Tonquin by W. Adams & Sons, and Shanghai by Baker & Co., see Snyder, 1997, p. 6. Two-handled Dish, $1,000.00 – 1,200.00.

PLATE 618. Shangay Plate, $175.00 – 200.00.

PLATE 619. **Shanghae**, J. Furnival & Co., Mark 53, circa 1845 – 1870. Sugar Bowl, $800.00 – 1,000.00, with lid.

PLATE 620. **Shanghai**, W. Adams & Sons, Mark 2a, circa mid-1800s. This is the same pattern as Tonquin by W. Adams & Sons, Shanghai by Baker & Co., and Shangay by an unidentified manufacturer. Plate, $175.00 – 200.00.

PLATE 621. **Shanghai**, W. H. Grindley & Co., Mark 60, circa 1891 – 1914. Plate, $125.00 – 150.00.

PLATE 622. **Shanghai**, unidentified manufacturer, Mark 116, circa after 1891. Cup and Saucer, $125.00 – 150.00.

PLATE 623. **Shapoo**, T. & R. Boote, Mark 20A, circa mid-1800s. Plate, $175.00 – 200.00.

PLATE 624. **Shapoo**, T. Hughes & Son, Mark 69, circa after 1910. Only the border design of the pattern is on this piece. See Williams I, p. 50 for the entire Shapoo pattern by Hughes. It is identical to the Shapoo pattern by T. & R. Boote. Cup and Saucer. $100.00 – 125.00.

PLATE 625. **Shell**, W. Adams & Co., Mark 7c, circa early 1900s. Plate, $70.00 – 85.00.

PLATE 626. **Shell**, E. Challinor, similar to Mark 30a, circa 1842 – 1867. Tea Pot, $1,200.00 – 1,400.00.

PLATE 628. **Shusan**, Mark 104A, F. & R. Pratt & Co., circa 1840s – 1850s. Platter, 18", $800.00 – 1,000.00.

PLATE 627. Shell by Challinor. Plate, $200.00 – 225.00.

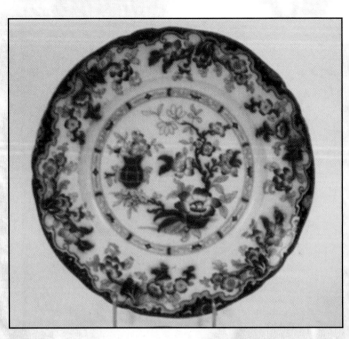

PLATE 629. **Simla**, marked "Imported by E. M. Forster & Co.," without pattern name, see Williams I, p. 50, circa 1860s, polychrome pattern. Plate, $125.00 – 150.00.

PLATE 630. **Simlay**, marked only with pattern name, see Mark 140, but attributed to Ridgways from an example having Ridgways' Bow & Quiver mark with "Stoke-on-Trent, England," circa after 1891, polychrome pattern, but the pattern is also found in monochrome Flow Blue. Plate, $125.00 – 150.00.

PLATE 631. **Simplex Pattern**, Booths, Mark 20Ba, circa after 1906. Plate, $50.00 – 65.00.

PLATE 632. **Singan**, attributed to Thomas Goodfellow, circa mid-1840s, see Williams III, p. 62. Handleless Cup, $150.00 – 175.00.

PLATE 633. "**Sloe Blossom**," see Snyder, 2000, p. 158, unmarked, circa mid-1800s. Cake Stand (pedestal base not visible), $500.00 – 600.00.

PLATE 634. **Sobraon**, unidentified manufacturer, Mark 139, circa mid-1800s. This is the same pattern as Chinese by Bourne & Leigh. Plate, $200.00 – 250.00.

PLATE 635. **Somerset**, W. H. Grindley & Co., Mark 61, circa 1914 – 1925. Platter, 16", $300.00 – 350.00.

PLATE 636. "**Spinach**," hand-painted pattern, Utzschneider & Co., French, Mark 146, circa late 1800s. Berry Bowl, $60.00 – 75.00. Plate (not shown), $125.00 – 150.00.

PLATE 637. "**Spinach**," hand-painted pattern, Libertas, Prussia, Mark 155, circa late 1800s. Plate, $125.00 – 150.00.

PLATE 638. **Stanley**, Johnson Bros., Mark 72, circa early 1900s. Plate, $70.00 – 85.00.

PLATE 639. "**Star with Gothic Trim**," unmarked, hand-painted pattern, see Williams III, p. 45, circa late 1800s. Plate, $150.00 – 175.00.

PLATE 640. **Sterling**, Johnson Bros. Mark 73, circa 1913 and after. Plate, $60.00 – 75.00.

206

PLATE 642. **Stratford**, Burgess & Leigh, Mark 24, circa 1891 – 1919. Chamber Pot, $400.00 – 500.00.

PLATE 641. **St. Louis**, Johnson Bros., Mark 70, circa early 1900s. Plate, $70.00 – 85.00.

PLATE 643. "**Strawberry Luster**," Mellor, Venables & Co., circa mid-1800s (see Williams I, p. 203). Pitcher, $400.00 – 500.00; Coffee Pot, $1,200.00 – 1,400.00.

PLATE 644. **Superior**, Petrus Regout, Dutch, Mark 153, circa early 1900s. Plate, $70.00 – 85.00.

PLATE 645. **Sydney**, New Wharf Pottery, similar to Mark 98, circa 1890 – 1894. Plate, $70.00 – 85.00.

PLATE 646. **Syrian**, W. H. Grindley & Co., Mark 60, circa 1891 – 1914. Pitcher, 7", $400.00 – 500.00.

PLATE 647. Syrian Wash Set. Bowl and Pitcher, $2,000.00 – 2,500.00; Covered Soap Dish, $250.00 – 275.00; Toothbrush Holder, $175.00 – 225.00.

PLATE 648. Syrian Covered Waste Jar, $1,000.00 – 1,200.00.

PLATE 649. **The Temple**, Podmore, Walker & Co., Mark 103, circa 1834 – 1859. Plate, $200.00 – 225.00.

PLATE 650. **Togo**, F. Winkle & Co., Mark 129, circa early 1900s. Plate, $125.00 – 150.00.

PLATE 652. Tokio by Johnson Bros. Plate, $100.00 – 125.00.

PLATE 651. **Tokio**, Johnson Bros., Mark 70, circa early 1900s. Covered Serving Dish, $350.00 – 400.00.

PLATE 654. Tokio by Johnson Bros. Gravy Boat and Tray, $225.00 – 275.00.

PLATE 653. Tokio by Johnson Bros. Cup and Saucer, $120.00 – 140.00.

PLATE 656. **Tonquin**, Clementson & Young, Mark 32, circa 1845 – 1847. Platter, 18", $1,200.00 – 1,400.00.

PLATE 655. **Tonquin**, W. Adams & Sons, Mark 1, circa 1840s. This pattern is like Shanghai by both W. Adams (see Mark 2a) and W. & T. Adams (see Mark 10a). It is also the same as Shanghai by Baker & Co., and Shangay by an unidentified manufacturer. Plate, $175.00 – 200.00.

PLATE 657. **Tonquin**, J. Heath, Mark 66, circa 1845 – 1853. Plate, $200.00 – 225.00.

PLATE 658. **Touraine**, Henry Alcock & Co., Mark 11, circa 1891 – 1900. This pattern is also found with a Stanley Pottery mark, see Mark 113, circa 1928 – 1931. That mark was used by the successor to Henry Alcock & Co., Colclough & Co. New reproductions of the Touraine pattern and the Stanley mark have been on the market for a few years. (See the Reproductions section at the end of the book). Soup Plate, $75.00 – 90.00.

PLATE 659. **Tower**, unmarked, circa early 1900s. See Williams II, p. 107. Plate, $125.00 – 150.00.

PLATE 660. **Trent**, Bishop & Stonier, Mark 20a, circa 1891 – 1910. Graduated Pitchers: 7", $350.00 – 400.00; 8". $400.00 – 450.00; 9", $450.00 – 500.00.

PLATE 661. **Trent**, New Wharf Pottery, Mark 100, circa 1890 – 1894. Plate, $75.00 – 90.00.

PLATE 662. **Trentham**, T. Rathbone, Mark 105, circa 1912 – 1923. Pitcher, 9", $300.00 – 400.00.

PLATE 664. **Tulip**, Johnson Bros., Mark 70, circa early 1900s. Covered Serving Bowl, $225.00 – 275.00.

PLATE 663. **Trilby**, Wood & Son, Mark 131, circa 1891 – 1907. Serving Bowl, $150.00 – 175.00.

PLATE 665. **"Tulip"** or **"Lustre Band,"** unmarked, hand-painted pattern, attributed to Elsmore & Foster, circa 1860s (see Williams II, p. 222 and Williams III, p. 64). Handleless Cup and Saucer, $175.00 – 200.00.

PLATE 666. **"Tulip & Sprig,"** unmarked, hand-painted pattern, circa early 1900s. (See Snyder, 1997, p. 132.) This is not the same hand-painted pattern as the one in Williams II, p. 227, with the same name. Plate, $125.00 – 150.00.

PLATE 667. **Turin**, Johnson Bros., Mark 73, circa 1913 and after. Platter, 12", $150.00 – 200.00.

PLATE 668. **Turkey/Wild Turkey**, Cauldon, similar to Mark 29, circa 1905 – 1920. Platter, 23", $1,000.00 – 1,200.00.

PLATE 669. **Turkey**, Doulton, Mark 44, circa early 1900s. Platter, 21", $800.00 – 1,000.00.

PLATE 670. **Turkey**, marked "Oliver China," American company in Sebring, Ohio, circa early 1900s. Platter, 20", $300.00 – 400.00.

PLATE 672. Turkey by Ridgways. Platter, 20", $800.00 – 1,000.00.

PLATE 671. **Turkey**, Ridgways, Mark 108, circa early 1900s. Plate, $125.00 – 150.00.

PLATE 673. **Turkey**, Villeroy & Boch, German, Mark 152a, circa early 1900s. Platter, 20", $800.00 – 1,000.00.

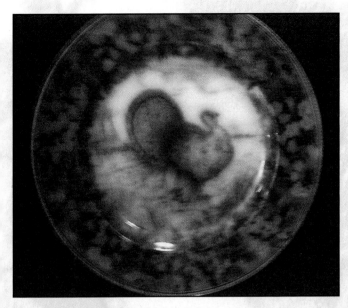

PLATE 674. **Turkey**, Josiah Wedgwood impressed name mark with date code for 1890. Plate, $125.00 – 150.00.

PLATE 675. **Turkey**, marked "France," circa after 1891. Platter, 20", $300.00 – 400.00.

PLATE 676. **Turkey**, unmarked, but the transfers are similar to the turkeys in Plate 675. Pair of Plates, $75.00 – 100.00 each.

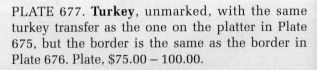

PLATE 677. **Turkey**, unmarked, with the same turkey transfer as the one on the platter in Plate 675, but the border is the same as the border in Plate 676. Plate, $75.00 – 100.00.

PLATE 678. **Turkey**, unmarked, but the border appears to be the same as the border on the platter in Plate 675. Plate, $75.00 – 100.00.

PLATE 679. **Turkey**, unmarked, circa early 1900s. Plate, $100.00 – 125.00.

PLATE 680. Turkey Platter, 20", matches Plate 679, $600.00 – 800.00.

PLATE 681. **Two Temples II**, Keeling & Co., Mark 77, circa 1886 – 1891. This pattern name is not a factory name, but the name is commonly used for this particular variation of the Blue Willow pattern. Plate, $150.00 – 175.00.

PLATE 682. **Tyne**, Bridgwood & Son, Mark 22A, circa early 1900s. Plate, $65.00 – 80.00.

PLATE 683. **U.S.S. Brooklyn**, The French China Co., American, Mark 162, circa early 1900s. Bowl, $225.00 – 275.00.

PLATE 684. **U.S.S. Maine**, The French China Co., American, Mark 162, circa early 1900s. Oval Bowl, $250.00 – 300.00.

PLATE 685. **Utopia**, Crescent Pottery Co., Trenton, New Jersey, American, Mark 160, circa early 1900s. Plate, $65.00 – 80.00.

PLATE 687. **Venice**, Bishop & Stonier, Mark 20b, circa 1891 – 1910. Mantel Set: Clock and pair of Vases, $4,000.00 – 5,000.00 set.

PLATE 686. **Vane**, Alfred Meakin, Ltd., Mark 86, circa early 1900s. Butter Pat, $35.00 – 40.00; Plate, (not shown), $70.00 – 85.00.

PLATE 688. **Venice**, Grimwade Bros., Mark 56, circa 1886 – 1900. Chamber Pot, $300.00 – 400.00.

PLATE 689. **Venice**, Johnson Bros., Mark 70, circa early 1900s. Covered Serving Dish, $275.00 – 325.00.

PLATE 690. **Venice**, Soho Pottery, Mark 112A, circa 1901 – 1906. Covered Serving Dish, $350.00 – 400.00; Tray, $175.00 – 225.00.

PLATE 691. **Venice**, Upper Hanley Pottery, Mark 115, circa 1895 – 1900. Plate, $70.00 – 85.00.

PLATE 692. **Ventnor**, manufacturer unidentified, pattern name printed within a fancy scrolled design with "England," circa after 1891. Platter, 16", $350.00 – 400.00.

PLATE 693. **Venus**, Till & Sons, Mark 114, circa 1891 – 1928. Platter, 18", $275.00 – 325.00.

PLATE 694. **Vermont**, Burgess & Leigh, Mark 26, circa 1891 – 1919. Tureen, $400.00 – 500.00.

PLATE 695. **Vernon**, Doulton, Mark 43, circa 1891 – 1902. Punch Bowl, $2,500.00 – 3,000.00.

PLATE 696. **Vernon**, Ford & Sons, Mark 52, circa 1908 – 1930. Tray, 14", $275.00 – 325.00.

PLATE 697. **Vernon**, Mellor & Co., American, Mark 165, circa late 1800s. Serving Bowl, $150.00 – 175.00.

PLATE 698. **Verona**, Ridgways, Mark 110, circa 1912 – 1920. Platter, 12", $250.00 – 300.00.

PLATE 699. **Verona**, Wood & Son, Mark 131, circa 1891 – 1907. Pitcher, 8", $500.00 – 600.00.

PLATE 700. **Versailles**, T. Furnival & Sons, impressed anchor and sword mark, circa 1878 – 1900. Covered Serving Bowl, $275.00 – 325.00.

PLATE 701. **Victoria**, Wood & Son, Mark 131, circa 1891 – 1907. Serving Bowl, $150.00 – 175.00.

PLATE 702. **Vienna**, Johnson Bros., Mark 70, circa early 1900s. Bowl and Pitcher Set, $2,500.00 – 3,000.00 set.

221

PLATE 704. Virginia by Maddock. Platter, 18", $400.00 – 500.00. Creamer, $225.00 – 275.00.

PLATE 703. **Virginia**, John Maddock, Mark 83, circa 1880 – 1896. Plate, $100.00 – 125.00.

PLATE 705. Virginia by Maddock. Covered Serving Dish, $325.00 – 375.00.

PLATE 706. **Vista**, G. L. Ashworth & Bros., Mark 19, circa 1862 – 1890. Plate, $175.00 – 200.00.

PLATE 708. **Warwick**, unmarked, attributed to Podmore, Walker & Co., circa 1834 – 1859. (See Williams II, p. 110.) Tea Pot, $1,200.00 – 1,400.00.

PLATE 707. **Waldorf**, New Wharf Pottery, Mark 98, circa 1890 – 1894. This is the same pattern as Luzerne by Mercer Pottery (American). This pattern and mark are being reproduced (see the last section of this book on Reproductions). Plate, $75.00 – 90.00.

PLATE 709. **Warwick**, Warwick China Co., American, circa early 1900s. Several Flow Blue patterns were made by the Warwick China Co., see Mark 167. The patterns are usually referred to as "Warwick," although popular names have evolved. See Snyder, 2000, pp. 140 and 141 for many of these popular names. (Some more examples are in Plates 710 – 720.) Warwick Tray, 10", in the "Calico" pattern, $275.00 – 325.00.

PLATE 710. Warwick Pitcher, 6", in the "Calico" pattern, $200.00 – 250.00.

PLATE 711. Warwick two-quart Pitcher in the "Calico" pattern, $500.00 – 600.00.

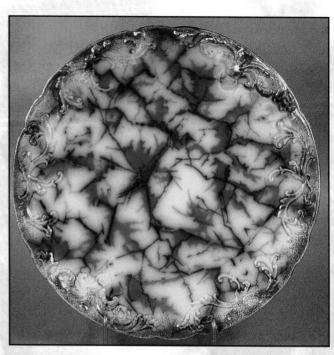

PLATE 712. Warwick Plate in the "Cracked Ice" pattern, $125.00 – 150.00.

PLATE 713. Warwick Jardiniere in the "Cracked Ice" pattern, $800.00 – 1,000.00.

PLATE 714. Warwick Butter Dish in the "Cracked Ice" pattern, $400.00 – 500.00.

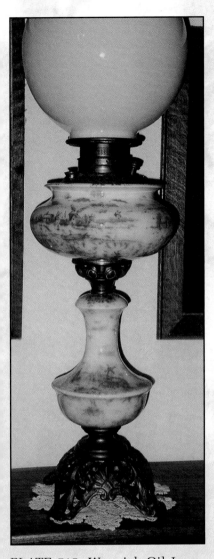

PLATE 716. Warwick Trivet in the "Pansy" pattern, $150.00 – 175.00.

PLATE 715. Warwick Oil Lamp in the "Delft" pattern, $1,000.00 – 1,200.00.

PLATE 717. Warwick Relish Dish in the "Pansy" pattern, $150.00 – 175.00.

PLATE 718. Warwick Syrup or Molasses Pitcher in the "Wild Rose" pattern, $500.00 – 600.00.

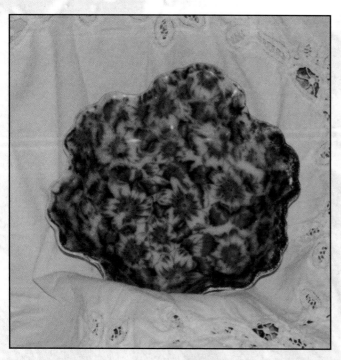

PLATE 719. Warwick Scalloped Dish in the "Wild Rose" pattern, $250.00 – 300.00.

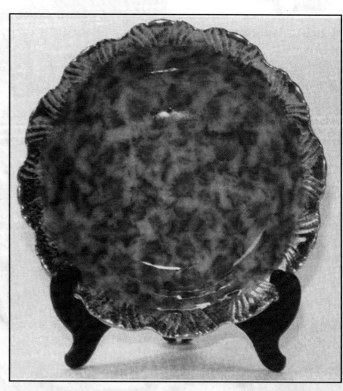

PLATE 720. Warwick Serving Bowl in the "Wild Rose" pattern, $150.00 – 175.00.

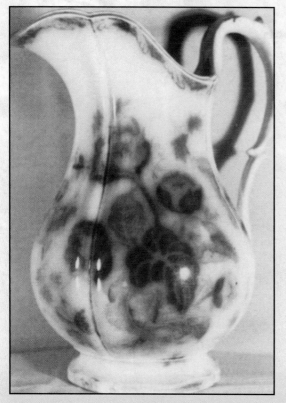

PLATE 721. **Water Nymph**, unmarked, the same pattern was made by Josiah Wedgwood during the early 1870s, according to Williams II, p. 166. Pitcher, 10", $700.00 – 800.00.

PLATE 722. **Watford**, Ford & Sons, Ltd., Mark 52a, circa early 1900s. Gravy Boat, $75.00 – 100.00.

PLATE 724. Watteau by Doulton, Mark 46, circa after 1930. Serving Dish, $500.00 – 600.00.

PLATE 723. **Watteau**, Doulton, Mark 43, circa 1891 – 1902. There are different scenes with a romantic theme in the Doulton Watteau patterns. The pattern continued to be made as late as the 1930s. Also, the Watteau pattern name was used if only the border design was applied. Plate, $125.00 – 150.00.

PLATE 725. Lid to Watteau Serving Dish in Plate 724.

PLATE 726. Watteau by Doulton, Mark 46, after 1930. Chocolate Pot, $600.00 – 700.00.

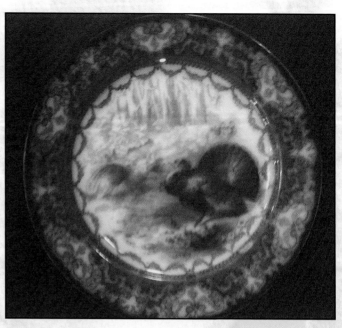

PLATE 727. Watteau by Doulton, Mark 41a, circa 1891 – 1902. Only the border pattern is on this example. Plate, $60.00 – 75.00.

PLATE 728. Watteau by Doulton, circa early 1900s. The border pattern is from the Watteau design, but the center pattern is a turkey. Plate, $125.00 – 150.00.

PLATE 729. **Watteau**, New Wharf Pottery, Mark 98, circa 1890 – 1894. This is the same pattern as the one made by Doulton. Platter, 11", $400.00 – 500.00.

PLATE 730. **Watteau**, Mark 141. This mark was unidentified for this pattern in my first edition. This mark has been found in conjunction with an impressed British Anchor and the date, September 1913, a mark attributed to the British Anchor Pottery Co., Ltd. (See Godden, p. 105.) Plate, $100.00 – 125.00.

PLATE 731. **Waverly**, W. H. Grindley & Co., Mark 60, circa 1891 – 1914. Gravy Boat, $100.00 – 125.00.

PLATE 732. **Waverly**, John Maddock, Mark 83, circa 1880 – 1896. Plate, $75.00 – 90.00.

PLATE 733. **Weir**, Ford & Sons, Mark 52, circa after 1908. Gravy Boat, $120.00 – 145.00.

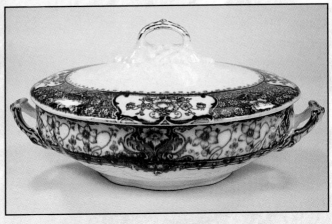

PLATE 734. **Welbeck**, Sampson Hancock & Sons, Mark 64, circa 1906 – 1912. Covered Serving Dish, $275.00 – 325.00.

PLATE 735. **Wellington**, J. & G. Meakin, similar to Mark 88, circa late 1800s to early 1900s. Bowl and Pitcher Set, $2,000.00 – 2,500.00.

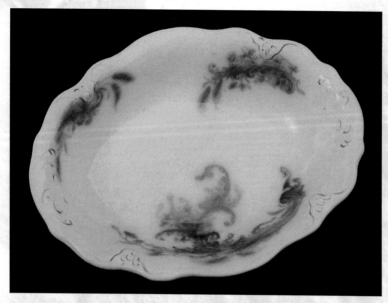

PLATE 736. **Wentworth**, J. & G. Meakin, Mark 89, circa late 1800s to early 1900s. Platter, 12", $125.00 – 150.00.

PLATE 737. **Whampoa**, Mellor, Venables & Co., circa 1830s. Coffee Pot, $1,400.00 – 1,600.00.

PLATE 738. Whampoa, unmarked, attributed to Mellor, Venables & Co., circa 1830s (see Williams I, p. 56 and II, p. 75). Pitcher, 7", $800.00 – 1,000.00.

PLATE 739. "**Wheel**," hand-painted pattern with copper luster, Charles Allerton & Sons, Mark 15, circa 1891 – 1912. (See Williams II, p. 228.) Pitcher, 8", $400.00 – 500.00.

PLATE 740. "**Wild Strawberry**," unmarked, hand-painted pattern, circa mid-1800s. (See Williams II, p. 228.) Plate, $125.00 – 150.00.

PLATE 741. **Willow**, Doulton, Mark 40, circa 1882 – 1890. Plate, $150.00 – 175.00.

PLATE 742. Willow by Doulton, Mark 41, circa 1891 – 1902. Cake Stand, $400.00 – 500.00.

PLATE 743. Willow by Doulton, Mark 42, circa 1891 – 1902. Creamers, $225.00 – 250.00 each.

PLATE 744. **Willow**, C. T. Maling, Mark 83A, circa 1908. Lamp Base, $500.00 – 600.00.

PLATE 745. **Willow**, unmarked, circa early 1900s. Tea Pot, $300.00 – 400.00.

PLATE 746. Willow Pitcher with the same pattern and made in the same mold as the previous tea pot. $300.00 – 350.00.

PLATE 748. **Wreath**, T. Fell & Co., circa mid-1800s. Egg Cup Holder, $1,000.00 – 1,200.00.

PLATE 747. **Windflower**, Burgess & Leigh, Mark 26, circa 1891 – 1919. Plate, $50.00 – 65.00.

PLATE 749. Exterior of Egg Cup Holder in the Wreath pattern.

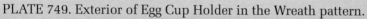

PLATE 750. **Yeddo**, Arthur J. Wilkinson, Mark 126, circa 1907. Soup Bowl, $100.00 – 125.00.

PLATE 751. **Yedo**, G. L. Ashworth, Marks 17 and 18, circa 1862 – 1890. Footed Platter, 13", $500.00 – 600.00.

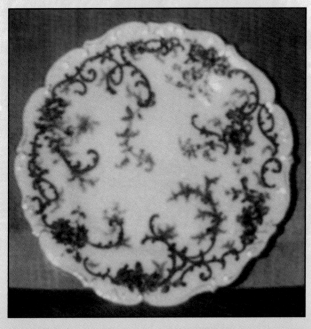

PLATE 752. **York**, marked "Cauldon, England," circa early 1900s (see Williams III, p. 60). This example is also marked with an importer's name, "Pitkin & Brooks, Chicago." Plate, $60.00 – 75.00.

PLATE 753. Floral pattern, by Charles Collinson & Co., Mark 33A, circa 1851 – 1873. Platter, 16", $600.00 – 800.00, mint condition.

PLATE 754. Floral pattern by Copeland, marked "Copeland, Late Spode," circa 1847 – 1867. "Late Spode" is not a pattern name but refers to Copeland's association with the earlier Spode factory. Serving Bowl, $250.00 – 300.00.

PLATE 756. Covered Serving Dish by Copeland, $700.00 – 800.00.

PLATE 755. Scenic pattern by Copeland, marked "Copeland Spode" (see Godden Mark 1074), circa 1875 – 1890. Tray, 14", $800.00 – 1,000.00.

PLATE 757. Serving Dish by Copeland, $1,000.00 – 1,200.00.

PLATE 758. Groups of flowers form this pattern, Copeland & Garrett, circa 1833 – 1847 (see Godden Mark 1091). Covered Serving Dish, $400.00 – 450.00; Plate, $125.00 – 150.00; Platter, 12", $300.00 – 350.00; Compote, $350.00 – 400.00.

PLATE 759. Scenic pattern by Doulton, Mark 43, circa 1891 – 1902. Plate, $125.00 – 150.00.

PLATE 760. Stylized floral pattern by Doulton, Mark 43, circa 1891 – 1902. Pitcher, 12", $600.00 – 700.00.

PLATE 761. Floral pattern by Samuel Johnson, circa late 1800s to early 1900s. Pitcher, 12", $400.00 – 500.00.

PLATE 762. Oriental scenic pattern by Knight Elkin & Co., see Godden Mark 2302, circa 1826 – 1846. Covered Serving Dish, $800.00 – 1,000.00.

PLATE 763. Interior of Plate 762.

PLATE 764. Floral pattern by Mintons, impressed marks with a year code for 1876. Platter, 23", $800.00 – 1,000.00.

PLATE 765. Floral pattern by T. Rathbone & Co., mark is similar to Mark 105, circa 1912 – 1923. Chamber Pot, $300.00 – 400.00.

PLATE 766. Floral pattern by William Ridgway & Co., marked "W. R. & Co., Opaque Granite," circa 1830 – 1834. One-handled Dish, $275.00 – 325.00.

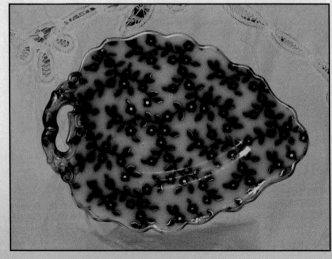

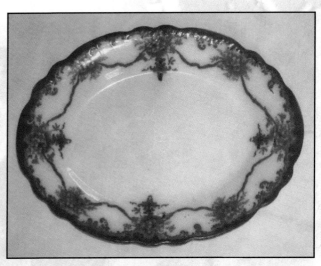

PLATE 767. Floral pattern by Upper Hanley Pottery, Mark 115, circa 1895 – 1900. Footed Covered Serving Bowl, $300.00 – 350.00.

PLATE 768. Matching Platter, 16", $275.00 – 325.00.

PLATE 769. Scrolled floral pattern by Josiah Wedgwood, with a year code for 1894. Plate, $100.00 – 125.00.

PLATE 770. Floral pattern by Wiltshaw & Robinson, Mark 127, circa early 1900s. Egg Holder with Handle, $300.00 – 400.00.

PLATE 771. Scrolled pattern, "TB" monogram mark, unidentified manufacturer, circa early 1900s. Cup and Saucer, $120.00 – 140.00.

237

PLATE 772. Bowl and Pitcher, hand-painted pattern of leaves and grapes with copper luster, unmarked, circa mid-1800s, $3,000.00 – 4,000.00 set.

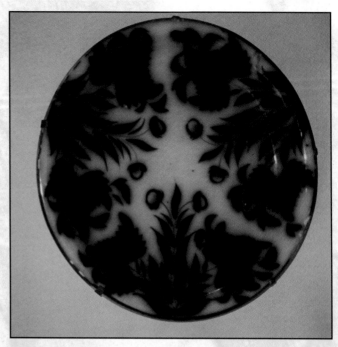

PLATE 773. Whey Bowl, 19", unmarked, hand-painted pattern of leaves and small pods, circa mid-1800s, $2,000.00 – 2,500.00.

PLATE 774. Serving Dish, 12", unmarked, hand-painted pattern of large stylized leaves around border and a small floral design in the center, circa mid-1800s, $500.00 – 600.00.

PLATE 775. Pitcher, 6", molded body designs of berries and leaves painted with dark cobalt blue accent the circus animal figural motif of elephants (camels are shown on the back) on this piece, circa mid-1800s, $700.00 – 800.00.

PLATE 777. Child's Tea Set decorated with Flow Blue borders overlaid with gold luster, circa late 1800s, $3,000.00 – 4,000.00 set.

PLATE 776. Pitcher, molded figural pattern of trees, flowers, and figures, highlighted with deep cobalt blue, circa mid-1800s, $800.00 – 1,000.00.

PLATE 779. Cheese Dish, floral pattern, circa early 1900s, probably American, $300.00 – 400.00.

PLATE 778. Child's Set of Tea Cups decorated with an overall pattern of berries, vines, and flowers, $150.00 – 175.00 each.

PLATE 780. Hot Water Plate on metal base, circa late 1800s, $250.00 – 350.00.

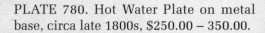

PLATE 781. Perfume Bottle, Oriental scenic pattern, circa late 1800s, $1,000.00 – 1,200.00.

PLATE 782. Another view of Perfume Bottle in Plate 781.

PLATE 784. Pitchers, floral pattern, circa early 1900s, probably American. Left, $100.00 – 125.00; right, $125.00 – 150.00.

PLATE 783. Cream Pitcher, floral pattern, circa early 1900s, $175.00 – 225.00.

Plate 785. Plate, Oriental scenic pattern featuring a willow tree, circa mid-1800s, $150.00 – 200.00.

PLATE 786. Plate, floral pattern featuring a large flower and leaves, circa mid-to-late 1800s, $125.00 – 150.00.

PLATE 787. Plate, stylized floral border pattern, circa early 1900s, $65.00 – 80.00.

PLATE 788. Plate, scrolled border pattern, circa early 1900s, $60.00 – 75.00.

PLATE 789. Platter, 12", floral pattern, circa mid-to-late 1800s, $400.00 – 500.00.

PLATE 790. Sauce Tureen and Tray, scrolled pattern, circa mid-to-late 1800s, $1,000.00 – 1,200.00 set.

PLATE 791. Sugar Bowl, Oriental scenic pattern, circa mid-to-late 1800s, $800.00 – 1,000.00, with lid.

PLATE 792. Tea Set, floral pattern distinguished by one large cluster of flowers and smaller clusters of flowers scattered over the surface, circa late 1800s. This pattern is very similar to Berlin Groups. Cake Plates, $175.00 – 225.00 each; Waste Bowl, $125.00 – 150.00; Tea Pot, $275.00 – 325.00; Cup and Saucer, $75.00 – 100.00; Sugar, $150.00 – 175.00; Creamer, $75.00 – 100.00.

PLATE 793. Pair of Vases, 12", floral and leaf pattern, circa 1900, $1,000.00 – 1,200.00 pair.

Reproductions

My first book on Flow Blue addressed the subject of current reproductions in the early 1980s. The Blakeney Pottery Limited, located at Stoke-on-Trent, England, in business since 1968, was offering wares termed "Victorian Reproductions." Mustache cups, shaving mugs, wash basins, pitchers, hatpin holders, and dresser trays were a few of the items decorated with a "flow blue" pattern of large blue roses. A few example were shown in my book. Unfortunately, Flow Blue reproductions did not remain confined to such pieces. Other fake marks and examples appeared during the late 1980s and early 1990s. In my *Second Series*, released in 1995, additional fake marks and objects with those marks were included.

That those marks and china were reproductions was obvious to the majority of Flow Blue collectors. They were more of a nuisance rather than a large problem. Today, though, the problem is growing because manufacturers are becoming bolder. Companies are more closely replicating authentic English pottery marks, pieces and decoration. The Blakeney Pottery marks shown in my earlier books consisted of a coat of arms, or a pattern name with "Flo Blue, T. M. Staffordshire."

Those marks did not incorporate a genuine factory name. Recent reproductions, however, use the names or initials of English factories, such as Dunn Bennet & Co., Stanley Pottery Co., and T. Rathbone. The marks closely duplicate those old factories' marks. The decoration and molds have become more sophisticated as well.

I hear often from purchasers of new Flow Blue. Mostly, their inquiries are seeking authentication of what they have bought. They fear that perhaps the pieces are reproductions. Chiefly because prices were low, they hope they have found a bargain. The best protection against purchasing reproductions is to be as knowledgeable as possible through study about, and contact with, the "old" Flow Blue. Be on the alert for new items, especially when a number of different objects are found with the same pattern. Remember low prices on such items are usually the best clue. Trust your instincts. Like the old adage, "If it seems too good to be true, it usually is not true." Although everyone likes to find a bargain, Flow Blue bargains are not very plentiful!

The following photographs illustrate a number of fake and misleading marks found on new and nonauthentic Flow Blue china.

PLATE 794. Mark A. Coat of Arms mark, Ironstone, Staffordshire, England. "Victoria" or "Romantic" as pattern names can be found with this mark. This is a mark used by the Blakeney Pottery Company, Stoke-on-Trent, England, on a variety of items with "flow blue" decoration. This mark and type of ware have been on the market since the 1980s. See Plates 795 – 797 which have the same floral rose pattern and this mark.

PLATE 795. Scuttle Shaving Mug, Pitcher, and Tray, Mark A.

PLATE 796. Wash Bowl, Mark A.

PLATE 797. Pitcher to Wash Set, Mark A.

PLATE 799. Bowl and Pitcher with a scenic pattern, Mark B.

PLATE 798. Mark B. Variation of the Coat of Arms mark with "Victoria Ware, Ironstone." This mark is on Plates 799 – 803.

PLATE 800. Interior of Wash Bowl.

PLATE 801. Platter with a scenic pattern, Mark B.

PLATE 802. Three Pitchers with a willow type scenic pattern, Mark B.

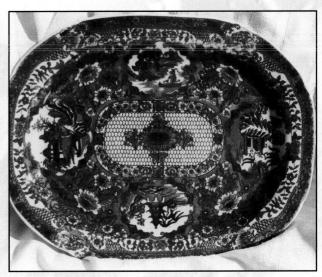

PLATE 803. Platter with a floral pattern and cameo Oriental scenes, Mark B.

PLATE 804. Mark C. Coat of Arms mark, Flow Blue.

PLATE 805. Chamber Pot, Mug, Soap Dish, and Toothbrush Holder, Mark C.

PLATE 806. Mark D. Coat of Arms Mark, Ironstone.

PLATE 807. High Top Shoe with floral pattern, Mark D.

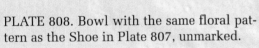
PLATE 808. Bowl with the same floral pattern as the Shoe in Plate 807, unmarked.

PLATE 809. Exterior of Bowl in Plate 808.

PLATE 811. Miniature or Toy Bowl and Pitcher Set in the same pattern as Plate 807, unmarked.

PLATE 810. Pitcher matching Wash Bowl in Plate 808, Mark D.

PLATE 812. Mark E. Homestead, Flow Blue mark.

PLATE 813. Bowl and Pitcher Set, scenic pattern, Mark E.

PLATE 814. Mark F. Coat of Arms Mark and Chelsea pattern name.

PLATE 815. Charger or Chop Plate, "Chelsea" floral pattern, Mark F.

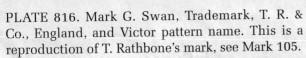

PLATE 816. Mark G. Swan, Trademark, T. R. & Co., England, and Victor pattern name. This is a reproduction of T. Rathbone's mark, see Mark 105.

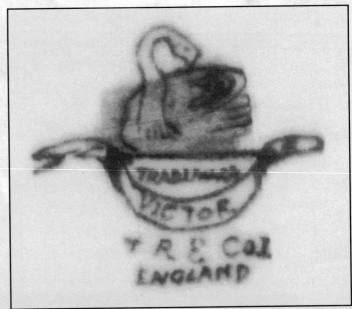

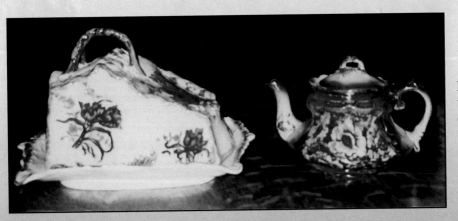

PLATE 817. Cheese Dish and Tea Pot with Mark G. The patterns are different but both have the pattern name "Victor."

PLATE 818. Mark H. Beehive mark, Imperial Semi China, Dunn Bennett & Co., Burslem and Iris pattern name. This is a new mark on chamber sets. This mark and the following photographs and information on the "Iris," "Waldorf," and Touraine" patterns and marks which are being reproduced on new china are courtesy of Mark Chervenka, editor, *Antique & Collectors Reproductions News*, the monthly newsletter on fakes and reproductions since 1992. Readers may contact him at www.repronews.com.

PLATE 819. Toothbrush Holder with "Iris" pattern, Mark H.

PLATE 820. Authentic Dun Bennet & Co. mark.

PLATE 821. Mark I. Crown and Staffordshire Bow Knot mark, New Wharf Pottery, Sem. Porcelain with Waldorf pattern name. Note the "i" is missing in "Semi-Porcelain." This is a new mark on cups and saucers.

PLATE 822. Cup with "Waldorf" pattern, Mark I.

PLATE 823. Authentic New Wharf Pottery mark.

PLATE 824. Mark J. Crown, Stanley Pottery Co., Touraine pattern name, and a registry number for 1898. This is a new mark found on various pieces of table china. "England," however is not included with the mark.

PLATE 825. Authentic Stanley Pottery Co. mark with "England."

Bibliography

Barber, William Atlee. *Marks of American Potters*, 1904.

Boger, Lousie Ade. *The Dictionary of World Pottery and Porcelain*. New York: Charles Scribner's Sons, 1971.

Brink, Mrs. William. *"Staffordshire," The Encyclopedia of Collectibles*. Alexandria, Virginia: Time-Life Books, 1980.

Chervenka, Mark. *Guide to Fakes & Reproductions, 3rd Edition*. Iola, Wisconsin: Krause Publications, 2003.

_____. "Real or Reproduction?" *Antique Trader*, February 11, 2004.

Copeland, Robert. *Spode's Willow Pattern and Other Designs After the Chinese*. New York: Rizzoli, 1980.

Coysh, A. W. *Blue and White Transfer Ware 1780 – 1840*. Rutland, Vermont: Charles E. Tuttle Company, 1971.

Cushion, J. P. *Handbook of Pottery and Porcelain Marks*. London: Faber and Faber, 1980.

Fisher, S.W. *English Pottery and Porcelain Marks*. Des Moines, Iowa: Wallace-Homestead Book Co., 1970.

Gaston, Mary Frank. *The Collector's Encyclopedia of Limoges Porcelain Marks*. Paducah, Kentucky: Collector Books, 1980.

_____. *Blue Willow, An Illustrated Value Guide*. Paducah, Kentucky: Collector Books, 1983.

_____. *The Collector's Encyclopedia of Flow Blue China*. Paducah, Kentucky: Collector Books, 1983.

_____. *The Collector's Encyclopedia of Flow Blue China, Second Series*. Paducah, Kentucky: Collector Books, 1994.

_____. *English China*. Paducah, Kentucky: Collector Books, 2002.

_____. *Gaston's Blue Willow*. Paducah, Kentucky: Collector Books, 2004.

Godden, Geoffrey A. *Encyclopedia of British Pottery and Porcelain Marks*. New York: Crown Publishers, 1964.

Hughes, G. Bernard. *The Collector's Pocket Book of China*. New York: Tandem Books, 1965.

_____. *English and Scottish Earthenware*. London: Abbey Fine Arts, n.d.

Hughes, Bernard and Therle. *The Collector's Encyclopedia of English Ceramics*. London: Abbey Library, 1968.

Kovel, Ralph M. and Terry H. *Dictionary of Marks*. New York: Crown Publishers, 1953.

_____. *Kovel's New Dictionary of Marks*. New York: Crown Publishers, 1986.

Lehner, Lois. *Ohio Pottery and Glass*. Des Moines, Iowa: Wallace-Homestead Book Company, 1978.

_____. *Lehner's Encyclopedia of U.S. Marks on Pottery, Porcelain & Clay*. Paducah, Kentucky: Collector Books, 1988.

Little, W. L. *Staffordshire Blue*. London: B. T. Batsford, Ltd., 1969.

Mankowitz, Wolf and Reginald G. Hagger. *The Concise Encyclopedia of English Pottery and Porcelain*. New York: Hawthorn Books, Inc., n.d.

Mason, Veneita. *Popular Patterns of Flow Blue China with Prices*. Des Moines, Iowa: Wallace-Homestead Book Company, 1982.

Mountfield, David. *The Antique Collectors' Illustrated Dictionary*. London: Hamlyn, 1974.

Nix, Thomas. *Abbie's Flow Blue Price Guide Survey, 1991 – 92*. Sentinel Publishing, February 1992.

Norbury, James. *The World of Victoriana*. London: Hamlyn, 1972.

Poche, Emanuel. *Porcelain Marks of the World*. New York: Arco Publishing Company, Inc., 1974.

Sandon, Henry. *Royal Worcester Porcelain From 1862 to the Present Day*. London: Barrie & Jenkins, 1973.

Snyder, Jeffrey B. *Flow Blue, A Collector's Guide to Pattern, History, and Values*. West Chester, Pennsylvania: Schiffer Publishing, Ltd., 1992.

_____. *Revised and Expanded 4th Edition*. Atglen, Pennsylvania: Schiffer Publishing, Ltd., 2003.

_____. *Historic Flow Blue*. Atglen, Pennsylvania: Schiffer Publishing, Ltd., 1994.

_____. *A Pocket Guide to Flow Blue*. Atglen, Pennsylvania: Schiffer Publishing, Ltd., 1995.

_____. *Fascinating Flow Blue*. Atglen, Pennsylvania: Schiffer Publishing, Ltd., 1997.

_____. *Flow Blue, A Closer Look*. Atglen, Pennsylvania: Schiffer Publishing, Ltd., 2000.

Van Buskirk, William H. *Late Victorian Flow Blue and Other Ceramic Wares*. Atglen, Pennsylvania: Schiffer Publishing, Ltd., 2002.

Williams, Petra. *Flow Blue China: An Aid to Identification*. Jeffersontown, Kentucky: Fountain House East, 1971.

_____. *Flow Blue China II*. Jeffersontown, Kentucky: Fountain House East, 1973.

_____. *Flow Blue China and Mulberry Ware*. Jeffersontown, Kentucky: Fountain House East, 1975.

Indexes
Numbers refer to plate numbers

INDEX TO MANUFACTURERS' INITIALS

INDEX TO AMBIGUOUS MARKS

Other Books by Mary Frank Gaston

Gaston's Blue Willow, Third Edition

#6320, 8½" x 11", 272 pgs., PB, $19.95

The Collector's Encyclopedia of Limoges
Porcelain, Third Edition

#5609, 8½" x 11", 456 pgs., HB, $29.95

American Belleek

Antique Brass & Copper

Collector's Guide to Art Deco, Second Edition

The Collector's Encyclopedia of English China

The Collector's Encyclopedia of Flow Blue China

The Collector's Encyclopedia of Flow Blue China, Second Series

Haviland Collectables & Objects of Art

Knowles, Taylor & Knowles China

The Collector's Encyclopedia of R. S. Prussia

The Collector's Encyclopedia of R. S. Prussia, Second Series

The Collector's Encyclopedia of R. S. Prussia, Third Series

The Collector's Encyclopedia of R. S. Prussia, Fourth Series

R. S. Prussia Popular Lines